GW01100177

MASONS AND MASONRY

MASONS AND MASONRY

A selection of feature articles
published by the
Grand Lodge of Scotland
in their Masonic Yearbooks from
1953–1972

Edited by
George Draffen of Newington

LONDON
LEWIS MASONIC

© 1983

First published in collected form in the
United Kingdom in 1983

Published by
LEWIS MASONIC, Terminal House,
Shepperton, Middlesex who are
members of the
IAN ALLAN GROUP
of Companies

Published with the approval of the
GRAND LODGE OF SCOTLAND in whose
Yearbooks these articles first appeared.

British Library Cataloguing in Publication Data
Masons and Masonry
1. Freemasons – Scotland
I. Draffen, George II. Scottish masonic yearbook
366'. 1'09411   HS597
ISBN 085318 131 4

All rights reserved. No part of this book may be
reproduced or transmitted in any form or by any
means, electronic or mechanical, including
photocopying recording or by any information
storage and retrieval system without permission
of the Publisher or the Grand Lodge of Scotland
in writing.

Made and printed in Great Britain by The Garden City Press Limited,
Letchworth, Hertfordshire SG6 1JS

Contents

The dates in parentheses refer to the Scottish Masonic Yearbook in which each article appeared.

1	Masonic Initiation – *J. Mason-Allan* (1970)	1
2	The Installed Master – *George Draffen* (1964)	17
3	The Dukes of Atholl and Freemasonry *W. G. Fisher* (1969	23
4	Robert Burns – Freemason *Fred J. Belford* (1955)	42
5	The Cable-Tow – *W. Graham Brown* (1965)	70
6	Basic Principles of Masonic Symbolism *C. G. Reigner* (1967)	77
7	Some Notes on the Mark Degree *F. E. Gould* (1971)	93
8	Freemasonry in Scotland in 1717 *George Draffen* (1968)	124
9	Rudyard Kipling – Freemason *Raymond Karter* (1961)	128
10	Sir Walter Scott – Freemason *Adam M. Mackay* (1958)	137
11	Lodge Mother Kilwinning No O *George Draffen* (1953)	154
12	A Missing Grand Master Mason *H. V. de Lorey* (1963)	160
13	Our Ritual: A Study in its Development *J. Mason-Allan* (1960)	173
14	On Ritual – *George Draffen* (1972)	193

ABBREVIATIONS USED IN SOME OF THE ARTICLES

A.Q.C – Ars Quatuor Coronatorum (The Transactions of the Quatuor Coronati Lodge No 2076, London)

S.C. – Scottish Constitution
G.M.M. – Grand Master Mason
M.M.M. – Mark Master Mason

THE GRAND LODGE OF SCOTLAND YEARBOOK
Brethren who require further information about the Yearbook or wish to obtain a copy, should contact the Grand Secretary, Freemasons' Hall, 96 George Street, Edinburgh EH2 3DH, Scotland.

QUATUOR CORONATI LODGE OF RESEARCH No 2076
Two of the articles in this book have been reprinted by kind permission of Quatuor Coronati Lodge, London, the Premier Lodge of Masonic Research. For further information about joining the correspondence circle brethren should contact The Secretary, Q.C. Correspondence Circle Ltd, 60 Great Queen Street, London WC2B 5BA.

MASONIC PUBLICATIONS
This book is just one from a large range that are published by LEWIS MASONIC. For a current list and catalogue write to LEWIS MASONIC, Terminal House, Shepperton TW17 8AS, Middlesex, England.

Preface

IN PRINCIPIO ERAT VERBUM. These four words appear over the entrance to the Library Quadrangle of St Andrews University – perhaps with the thought that the beginning of knowledge is to be found in the written or printed word. Something of that same thought must have been in the minds of the members of the Publications Committee when the Grand Lodge of Scotland decided to publish a year book. From the very first issue the Yearbook of the Grand Lodge of Scotland has been 'different'. It contains, as one might expect, the usual lists of lodges, Provincial and District Grand Lodges, dates of lodge meetings and all the important data to be found in a reference book.

But it also carries articles of the type usually to be found only in the pages of the transactions of lodges of research such as the Quatuor Coronati Lodge, the Manchester Lodge for Masonic Research and other lodges of a like nature. Scotland has no lodge of research publishing transactions and the advent of a Yearbook seemed to the members of the Publications Committee to provide an admirable opportunity of disseminating masonic knowledge of freemasonry, not only within Scotland but throughout the world, to the members of the Scottish Craft. For every Scottish Master Mason receives a copy when he is presented with his Diploma as a Master Mason.

For thirty years this policy has been maintained and well over a hundred articles and papers on almost every aspect of freemasonry have appeared in the pages of the Yearbook. As a glance at the list of contents will show the articles vary widely in style and appeal. From the collected articles the publishers have chosen a selection which, in their opinion, have the widest appeal to freemasons in general. Many well known masonic authors are to be found in these pages and since all the editions, except the first, have long been out of print this book gives the reader an opportunity which he cannot get in any other way of reading articles which are not otherwise available.

It may be added that the Yearbook is available to any regular freemason on payment of the subscription and is usually published during the month of February every year.

Balmullo,
St Andrews, 1983 George Draffen

1
MASONIC INITIATION
J. Mason-Allan

I SHOULD AT the outset make it clear that by 'Initiation' is meant the ceremonial introduction of a qualified aspirant into a new sphere of knowledge and experience; and the word further implies that the ceremony by which the aspirant is so introduced is, potentially at least, quickening and vitalising in its effects upon the aspirant. The significance of this conception of Initiation will become clearer as my paper proceeds.

I begin by quoting one of the questions and answers that I had to learn after I had been admitted EA and before I could be passed FC.

Q. What is Freemasonry?
A. Freemasonry is a peculiar system of morality veiled in allegory and illustrated by symbol.

With that definition of freemasonry we have been so familiar from the beginning that many of us have scarcely taken the time to study what it means and implies – we have learned the words by heart and left the matter there. I do not propose to attempt now a detailed examination of its meaning. That 'morality' here has a wider significance than the same word in our everyday language will be taken for granted. The significance of the reference to allegory and symbol is obvious to all who are familiar with our ceremonials. In what sense and to what extent our system is 'peculiar' may be an intriguing problem for those who have the aptitude and inclination for such a study. The word in the definition to which I wish meantime to direct particular attention is the word 'system', for I think it is very important to grasp the implication of this word in this particular setting. That implication is, that though in our Craft we have three distinct ceremonies of Initiation – the ceremonies of Entering, Passing and Raising – these three ceremonies constitute an organic unity, in which not only each ceremony, but each element in each ceremony, is necessary for the completeness and harmony of the whole. You will remember that, after the candidate in the third degree has taken the obligation, the master says that it is, at that point, his duty to call the candidate's attention to a retrospect of those degrees through which he has already passed, in order that he may be the better enabled to appreciate the system as a whole, and the interdependency of its several parts. That our three degrees do constitute an organic unity is an important point to grasp early in our study of masonic initiation.

The next point I want to make, a very simple one, is that the symbolism of our ceremonies is derived from operative masonry and the craftsman's tools and equipment; and that the allegories in our ceremonies are concerned with a particular branch of building – Temple-building. But we are clearly taught that, under a veil of allegory and symbol, we are really concerned with the building of a spiritual temple, a 'temple not made with hands, eternal in the heavens'. More than that, while we are all concerned with the erection of such a spiritual temple, each of us is individually responsible for the preparation of one particular stone for its appropriate place in that temple – and that stone is our own personality.

The key to my own conception of what masonic initiation means, from the individual point of view, is the broad conception that the raw material on which the craftsman works and exercises his skill is the rough stone as taken from the quarries; that the aim and object of all his labours is to transform that rough stone into a perfect ashlar fitted for its proper place in the Holy Temple; and that the true interpretation of this symbolism is, that the rough stone as taken from the quarries represents the craftsman's imperfect personality as it is by nature before he begins his masonic task, and that the finished ashlar – which is the same stone, with all superfluous knobs and excrescences knocked off, and then squared and dressed – is his perfected personality, purified, disciplined, developed and fitted for its place in a spiritual temple. This is the broad conception that has been behind, and has actuated, my own study of masonry, a study that has been more or less continuous for just over thirty years.

I would now like to go back to the beginning of a craftsman's experiences as such, and the first point I should like to mention is a simple and obvious fact, which all craftsmen know, but which is symbolical of a deeper spiritual fact to which probably few have given thought. The simple and obvious fact is, that when a candidate first joins the craft, he leaves the multitude of the outside world who are not masons, and joins the few within a lodge which is adequately protected, by outer and inner guards, against any intrusion from the outside world. And further, having been admitted into the lodge, he there receives instruction that is withheld from those who are without and which for this reason is called 'esoteric'. That word esoteric is an interesting word that means much to those who have had experiences that have awakened them to its real significance, though it may mean very little to those who have not had such experiences. For example, the esoteric instruction given in the lodge – that is esoteric in respect that it is withheld from those in the outside world – is in very great measure given under veil of allegory and illustrated by symbol. The interpretation and understanding of these allegories and symbols are not so much matters of intellectual study as matters of life and experience (and this, indeed, is true of all true masonic progress); and when one brother has made such progress in experience as has given him a key to the understanding of some symbolism in the ceremony, while the brother sitting beside him lacks both the experience and the understanding, the former brother has acquired knowledge that is truly esoteric, not because it is withheld from the brother sitting next him but because it is beyond that brother's grasp until he too has made the progress and had the experiences that bring further enlightenment.

When the young EA is informed that there are several degrees in freemasonry, with peculiar secrets restricted to each, he is told a simple fact which is at the same time a symbol of a deeper fact – namely that even among brethren of the same degree there may be some who have knowledge that others lack, not because it is withheld, not because it is beyond their potential capacity to grasp and understand, but simply because they have not yet had the experiences necessary to quicken that potential capacity and make it actual.

All this may sound very difficult to some, while to others it may be not so difficult – indeed, rather simple and obvious. But from the point of view of masonic initiation it is rather fundamental, because it is the enlightenment that comes from such experience rather than the intellectual knowledge that comes from much study, that constitutes true initiation.

Still considering the beginnings of a craftsman's career as such, the next point to note is, that before one can be received into a masonic lodge he must be a fit and proper person to be so received. And we are taught that, to be a fit and proper person to be made a mason, a man must be of mature age, sound judgment and strict morals. Even at this stage these last two words should not be interpreted in the narrow, limited sense in which they are ordinarily used, but as covering the whole range of a man's conduct toward his fellowmen and the motives that inspire and guide his conduct. Since a candidate must have manifested a high ethical standard before he is qualified for admission to a lodge of freemasons, it follows that the further instruction he receives within the lodge must be something above and beyond such purely mundane ethics. This is but to repeat the point that I have already mentioned as taken for granted, namely, that when we speak of freemasonry as a 'peculiar system of morality' this word 'morality' must have a wider significance than the same word has in our everyday language, must mean more than the 'strict morals' in respect of which a candidate must be fully qualified before he is a fit and proper person to be made a mason.

Assuming that a man has made application for admission to a lodge, and that the master and other experienced brethren with a full sense of their responsibility in this matter (known in Scotland as the Enquiry Committee), are satisfied that he is fully qualified in the sense I have just indicated, before he can be admitted he must be 'properly prepared'. According to the questions and answers relating to the EA degree from which I have already quoted – questions and answers that are used in most lodges but unfortunately not in all lodges in Scotland – this preparation is said to be of a two-fold character. There is, of course, the purely physical preparation with which we are all familiar: but this is preceded by an inner preparation. Let me repeat the first two questions and answers:

Q. Where were you first prepared to be made a Mason?
A. In my Heart.
Q. Where next?
A. In a convenient room adjoining the Lodge.

While we are all familiar with the preparation that is effected in the convenient room adjoining the lodge, few, I fear, give much thought to the previous preparation that is assumed to have been effected by the candidate himself in the secrecy of his own heart. We are nowhere told in so many words what the nature of this preparation is supposed to have been; but I would suggest that we can get a clue to this if we study carefully the questions that the master addresses to the candidate after the latter has crossed the threshold of the lodge and before he is instructed to advance to the P . . . of L . . ., – assuming, of course, that the candidate's answers are given sincerely, that the points they cover represent his deep and considered convictions, and that they come readily to his lips as answers to the master's questions because they were among the matters passed under review in the secrecy of his heart, preparatory to his coming forward for Initiation.

In the first place, he declares to be a free man, and of the full age of twenty-one years – these are both points of simple fact.

Then he professes his belief in God, and further declares that he puts his trust in God in all times of difficulty and danger.

He declares that he has come forward for Initiation of his

own free will and accord; that he has not been influenced by any mercenary or other unworthy motive – in other words, that he has not come because he hopes to get any advantage, in business or otherwise, from his connection with the Craft; that his real reasons for coming forward are a genuine desire for knowledge and a sincere wish to render himself more extensively serviceable to his fellowmen; and that, impelled by these worthy motives, he seeks admission to the Masonic Craft because he has conceived a favourable opinion of the institution, and believes that it will be able to help him to the attainment of the ends he has in view – the acquisition of knowledge, and service of his fellowmen.

These are declarations that you and I have all made in open lodge, and if they reflect a genuine preparation that was effected in our hearts before we came forward for Initiation, then we were indeed 'properly prepared' to take full advantage of our masonic ceremonials as means of true Initiation.

Whether these ceremonials result in a true and genuine Initiation depends on two things – first, whether the candidate is in fact fully prepared to take advantage of the opportunities that the ceremonials and the instructions given in them offer to him; and second, whether he sincerely and persistently strives to carry out the instructions that he so receives and to manifest the masonic ideals in every department and aspect of his life.

Let me deal for a moment, and briefly, with one aspect of the instruction that the candidate receives as he passes through the three craft degrees – and this is a most important aspect from the point of view of my present thesis. In each degree the candidate is presented with working tools and instructed as to their use. These working tools are, in our speculative system, regarded as symbols, and when the candidate is presented with them he is given certain elementary but nevertheless important interpretations of them. But the working tools, as symbols, have deeper meanings and implications than those communicated in explicit terms by the brother who presents them. One of the tools presented to an EA is the Common Gavel or the Mallet, and one of the lessons deduced from it is that 'labour is the lot of man'. 'The heart may conceive and the head devise in vain if the hand be not prompt to execute the design'. And, as working tools are presented to the craftsman in all the craft degrees, it can be inferred that throughout the whole of the journey or process symbolised by these degrees, labour, sustained and persevering labour, is ideally and should be actually a characteristic of the true and conscientious craftsman.

I referred earlier to the craftsman having left the multitude in the outside world, and having joined the few within the lodge. Let me now emphasise that, having done so, he has put his hands to a task that demands not only special and sustained efforts but efforts that are not demanded of those of the outside world. A young officer in the first World War was made a mason, and after he had been raised he, rather proudly, communicated the fact to the officer commanding his battalion, who was a Provincial Grand Master under the English Constitution. What may have been the motives of the officer in telling the OC of his admission to the Craft or what response he expected from the OC I do not know, but I do know that the OC listened attentively until the young officer had said all he wanted to say, then quietly congratulated him, assuring him that he had taken a step that he would never regret, but concluded by solemnly and seriously pointing out to the young man that he (the OC) would judge all the young officer's work and actions by a higher standard than he would judge those of his brother officers who had not had the privilege of receiving the light of masonry and being instructed in those ideals that are inculcated within a masonic lodge. This story was told me by the young officer himself, and I repeat it here only to illustrate the point I want to make, namely, that he who has received the benefit of Masonic Initiation has not only received a great privilege, but has also thereby come under greater responsibilities than those who have not received similar enlightenment.

Masonry is a progressive science. When the candidate is so informed, in the south-east corner of the FC Lodge, the instruction has reference primarily to the progress he has made in being passed from one degree to another. But the words are true in a wider, and if I may say so, a more intimate and personal sense. Quite early in his masonic career, the Apprentice is exhorted to make a daily advance in masonic knowledge. Naturally the first step in carrying out this exhortation is to become thoroughly familiar with the ceremonies of the various degrees, and with the clear, explicit instructions communicated in them. These explicit instructions are the first masonic lessons to be learnt, and they form the basis of the profounder knowledge that will be acquired later, when the candidate learns to interpret the symbols and allegories that are embodied in the ceremonies. These primary instructions, also, are such as would command the immediate assent of every decent-living and right-thinking man. But for the craftsman, mere intellectual assent is not enough. To fulfil the purposes for which he was initiated into the Craft, he must assimilate these instructions into his very being, and apply them in practice in his daily life.

This last is not always easy. Indeed, it is sometimes very difficult to act according to our masonic principles in a world in which we may have to deal with men who are not actuated by the same lofty ideals and principles. Nevertheless we do have a responsibility to adhere as strictly and faithfully as we can to all our principles no matter what the cost may be. Is not this driven home to us in an unforgettable way in the culminating theme of our craft ceremonies, when we have set before us a noble and outstanding example of unshaken fidelity in a supreme test? Not many of us are called upon to face such supreme trials, but in our everyday life, in the course of 'the trivial round, the common task', we come up against many small matters that do try us and prove us. And accordingly we should cultivate such habits of heart and mind, such habits of vigilence, that we are always ready to meet these apparently small 'trials and probations', even when they come upon us suddenly and without warning (as they usually do); for it is only 'by repeated trials and probations, and a readiness at all times to undergo an examination' (that is, to meet an unexpected test) that we really know and prove ourselves to be true freemasons.

These trials and probations do not always come to us from outside – indeed even when they seem to come from outside they really come from within ourselves. It is true that our circumstances, our surroundings, provide the occasion of our being tried and proved, but the result of the test is determined by our own reactions to these circumstances.

When dealing with this distinction between the objective world outside ourselves, and the subjective world within, it is very important from the point of view of our present subject, 'Masonic Initiation', that we should understand what freemasonry teaches its candidates regarding their inner or subjective life, and their responsibilities in relation thereto. In an attempt to reach such an understanding, I would like to suggest that one valid interpretation of our leaving the outside world and entering a lodge, regarding this as a symbolical act, is that it represents our withdrawing from the objective material world around us, which we can contact and of which we can have experience only through our five physical senses, and our entering into the subjective, inner world of our own souls, of which we have a more immediate experience. This, I know, sounds very abstruse and difficult, and in a way it is. But at the same time, what I am trying to express in words, and what I find very difficult to express clearly in words, is something of which we have all had some direct experience, and therefore which we may recognise in essence. Perhaps what I am trying to get across will become clearer as we proceed.

I used the expression 'subjective, inner world of our own souls'. I might have used the word 'worlds', in the plural, because subjectively man lives in various 'worlds', between which there may be some degree of conflict.

In the first place a man has within him a world of emotion, wherein he experiences pleasure and sorrow, attraction and repulsion, desire and aversion. This is the sphere of his instincts, his appetites, his passions, in which he knows 'good' and 'evil', the world of 'moral' standards.

In the second place, man has within him a world of reason, in which he exercises his intelligence in his efforts to come to a clear understanding of Truth – the world of 'intellectual' standards.

And in the third place there is within man a spiritual world, which is alike beyond the 'good' and 'evil' of the emotional world and beyond the limitations of the intellectual world – the world of 'spiritual' standards.

I think I may say that all of us can, from personal experience, recognise the first two of these worlds – though we may not always distinguish clearly between them – and many of us have had indubitable experience of the third also. But would I be justified in saying that the instruction we received in the three craft degrees clearly set before us these three subjective worlds – for you will remember that I said at the beginning that I would try to found my thesis on what I was taught as I went through the three degrees? I think that the answer is definitely in the affirmative – indeed the three degrees themselves deal successively with these three subjective worlds – the moral, the intellectual, and the spiritual.

This is clearly indicated in the 'retrospect' which the master gives to the candidate in the third degree, from which I have already quoted. You will remember that, after recounting briefly some of the lessons inculcated in the first degree, the master continues: 'but above all it taught you to bend with humility and resignation to the will of T.G.A.O.T.U., and to dedicate your heart, thus purified from every baneful and malignant passion, and fitted for the reception of truth and wisdom, to His Glory and to the welfare of your fellow creatures'.

The words I want to emphasise are, first, 'thus purified from every baneful and malignant passion'. This very clearly indicates the intention of the instruction given in the first degree. It corresponds to the first stage of the ancient mysteries, known as 'catharsis' or purification.

Secondly, this process of catharsis or purification is preparatory to the next stage of the path, for it is a further intention of the work of the first degree that the heart, thus purified, may be 'fitted for the reception of truth and wisdom'. And when we pass on to the next stage of the path, the work of the first degree is not past and done with, for, in the 'retrospect', the master says: 'Proceeding onwards, still guiding your steps by the principles of moral truth'. Note these significant words, 'principles of moral truth'.

Here, then in the ritual itself, is clear and categorical instruction that the first degree is concerned with the principles of moral truth, and that its object is to purify the heart from every baneful and malignant passion; and the clear inference is, that its sphere of operation is the first of the three subjective worlds to which I have referred.

That the second degree is concerned with the second of these three worlds is even more clearly stated. In the retrospect the master says: 'Proceeding onwards . . . you were led in the second degree to contemplate the intellectual faculties, and to trace their development through the paths of heavenly science, even to the Throne of God Himself. The secrets of Nature and the principles of intellectual truth were then unfolded to your view'. On this I do not think that any further argument is necessary to demonstrate my point. This degree corresponds to the second stage of the Ancient Mysteries – that of Illumination.

But even when the heart has been purified and the intellect enlightened, there is still a further stage of progress ahead of the candidate – he still has to pass through the profoundly significant experience of the third degree. This, of course, is not dealt with in the retrospect, as are the other two degrees, for at that stage of the ceremony the culminating experience is still ahead of the candidate. But a little reflection on the significant ceremony of the third degree will enable us to recognise that its theme is really that of regeneration – the 'dying' to our lower selves, and being 'raised' to a plane that is above both the moral and the intellectual worlds, that is, to a spiritual plane, to the third and highest of the three subjective worlds to which I have referred.

This corresponds to the third and culminating stage of Initiation in the ancient mysteries, and it is significant to note that in these mysteries the instruction in this culminating stage was imparted in a dramatic form, in which the candidate took the part of a tutelary hero or deity who was put to death and restored again to life.

It would be easy to demonstrate my interpretation of the real meaning of our third degree conclusively from a detailed examination and exposition of the ritual of the degree itself, but that would take a longer time than I have at my disposal – indeed it would be an adequate subject for a separate and perhaps a fairly long paper by itself. So I shall content myself with the very brief statement that I have made, only adding that I remember very vividly that, when I was myself going through the third degree, and was l . . . at the d . . . l . . ., there came into my mind the scriptural text 'Therefore we are buried with Him by baptism into death; that like as Christ was raised up from the dead by the glory of the Father, even so we also should walk in newness of life'. (ROM. vi. 4.)

If you accept my very brief statement of the significance of our third degree, and accept also my averment that it could be fully substantiated by a detailed examination of the ritual of the degree, I think you will agree that I have demonstrated , on the basis of our rituals alone, that our three craft degrees are related to the three subjective worlds – the moral, the intellectual and the spiritual. And I would add, as a necessary corollary, that the instructions given in the three degrees, veiled in allegory and illustrated by symbol, are related to work that the craftsman has to carry out in these subjective realms of his own personality.

Is not what we are taught in the first degree on all fours with the exhortation of the writer on the Epistle to the Hebrews (HEB. xii. 1) 'Let us lay aside every weight, and the sin which doth so easily beset us', or the more detailed exhortation of St Paul to the Christians at Colossae (COL. iii., 8–10) 'But now ye also put off all these; anger, wrath, malice, blasphemy, filthy communication out of your mouth. Lie not one to another seeing ye have put off the old man with his deeds; and have put on the new man, which is renewed in knowledge after the image of Him that created him' (i.e. the 'new man')?

And are not the principles of the second degree, in which we 'contemplate the intellectual faculties and trace their development through the paths of heavenly science, even to the throne of God Himself' reflected in the words of St Paul to the church at Rome (ROM. xii., 2) 'Be not conformed to this world, but be ye transformed by the renewing of your minds that ye may prove what is that good, and acceptable, and perfect will of God'; in his words to the Phillipians (PHIL. ii., 3) 'Let this mind be in you which was also in Christ Jesus'; and in his exhortation to the church at Thessalonica (I. THESS. v., 21) to 'prove all things and to hold fast that which is good'; as well as in the exhortation of St Peter (I. PET. iii., 15) to 'be ready always to give answer to every man that asketh you a reason for the hope that is in you'?

Finally, when Nicodemus was told 'except a man be born again he cannot see the Kingdom of God', adding by way of explanation that 'except a man be born of water and of the Spirit, he cannot enter into the Kingdom of God', for 'that which is born of the flesh is flesh and that which is born of the Spirit is spirit' (see JOHN iii., 3, 5 and 6) was he not being referred to that profound spiritual experience which is symbolically enacted in our third degree? And is not corroboration of this, as well as confirmation of the particular form in which this teaching is presented in the ceremony of our third degree, to be found in the first scriptural text that I quoted, as well as in various other passages in which St Paul deals with the identification of the Christian with Christ in His death and resurrection. The necessity for this 'new birth' arises out of the incapacity of the natural man to 'see' or to 'enter into' the Kingdom of God. St Paul in many passages alludes to the distinction between the 'natural man' and 'spiritual man', and in one passage (I. COR. ii., 14) he says that 'the natural man receiveth not the things of the Spirit of God, for they are foolishness unto him; neither can he know them, for they are spiritually discerned'.

Thus, as I said, my interpretation of the three craft degrees that constitute the path of masonic initiation is consistent with and is corroborated by the fundamental principles of the Christian doctrine. No doubt I was influenced in my interpretation of the craft degrees by the Christian instruction I had received long before I became a mason; but nevertheless I think it is demonstrable, and I have tried to demonstrate, briefly and perhaps inadequately, that the scopes of our masonic degrees and that of Christian doctrine are identical. And I likewise have no doubt that our Jewish, Parsee or Muslim brethren, who would not so naturally as I did interpret masonic symbolism in terms of the Christian faith, could arrive at an interpretation in terms of their own respective faiths that would involve the same practical results.

I may say, too, that the three masonic degrees correspond to the three stages of the path of Christian mysticism as expounded in our extensive mystical literature apart from the canonical scriptures – Purification, Illumination and Union. And they also correspond to the three Paths to Union with God according to Eastern esotericism – the Path of Action or of Good Works (karma marga), the Path of Knowledge (jnana marga), and the Path of Spiritual Devotion (bhakti marga). And I have also tried to indicate that they correspond to the three stages of Initiation in the ancient mysteries.

I have only one more point to make, but to me it is a point of fundamental importance. I have already quoted part of the 'retrospect' in which the master says – 'Proceeding onwards, still guiding our steps by the principles of moral truth, we were led in the second degree to contemplate the intellectual faculties', and I pointed out that when we pass to the second degree, the work of the first degree is not a work that is past and done with. Similarly, when we pass to the third degree, we should continue to guide our steps by the principles of moral truth and also the principles of intellectual truth – these principles, in both the moral and intellectual worlds, being illuminated by the principles of spiritual truth inculcated in the third degree. More than that, though we leave the objective, outside world when we enter the lodge where we receive instructions that are related to the three subjective worlds, we return to the outside world, where our ordinary, everyday lives should be actuated and guided by the principles inculcated within the lodge. Thus the integrated personality of the craftsman functions in four worlds altogether – the material, the moral, the intellectual and the spiritual.

In the ceremony of the opening of the lodge in the third degree we are told that there is a point from which a Master Mason cannot err, that that point is 'with the centre', and that the centre is a point within a circle from which all parts of the circumference are equidistant.

Here we have a significant piece of symbolism of which no interpretation is given, or even hinted at, in the ceremony of the degree. But a clue to its interpretation is given in the Lecture on the tracing board of the first degree, which deals with the correct furnishing of a masonic lodge. The lecture says: 'In all well-formed and regularly constituted lodges there is a point within a circle from which a mason cannot err. This circle is bounded on the north and south by two grand parallels, the one representing Moses and the other King Solomon'.

Now Moses was the giver of the Moral Law, and in this setting may he not be regarded as an appropriate symbol of the Principles of Moral Truth? And King Solomon was famed for his wisdom, and may be regarded as an equally appropriate symbol of the Principles of Intellectual Truth.

The proper place for this symbol in a well-formed lodge is on the front of the Altar, the ideal shape of which is a perfect cube. On the Altar rests the VSL, which is a most appropriate symbol of the principles of Spiritual Truth. And as the front of the Altar is a square the circle will touch the VSL.

At the bottom the circle touches the checkered pavement, representing the earth, a symbol of the material world, the outside world where the craftsman lives his life of activity amongst his fellow men, including those who are not masons.

Thus the four sides of the square symbolise the four worlds, material, moral, intellectual and spiritual. And the circumference of the circle touches all four sides, and the centre, the point within the circle from which all parts of the circumference are equidistant, is likewise equidistant from all four of the bounding sides, which symbolise the four worlds. And this is the point from which a MM cannot err.

Does not this surely teach us that the point from which a MM cannot err is a point from which he, an integrated personality, living his life according to the principles that he has been taught within the lodge, governs and regulates his activities in all four worlds according to these principles? If he leaves this point his life may become one sided and unbalanced, characterised by excessive attention to one or other of these worlds to the neglect of the others – that is, by excessive activity, or excessive emotionalism, or excessive intellectualism, or excessive 'other worldliness'. His life in all four worlds should receive due care and cultivation, keeping each in true perspective, and recognising the proper limits and proportions of each. Thus will his life as a whole be balanced, symmetrical; thus may his personality become a perfect ashlar fitted for its proper place in the spiritual temple. This is my personal view of the aim of Masonic Initiation.

2
THE INSTALLED MASTER

George Draffen

IN ALMOST EVERY organisation the transference of authority by the presiding officer to his successor in office is accompanied by some ceremony. It may be nothing more than the President of the Golf Club removing from his own shoulders the badge of office and his placing it, with a few appropriate words, upon the shoulders of his successor. The inauguration of a Lord Provost, the enthronement of a Bishop and the induction of a Judge are naturally more elaborate. The coronation of a Sovereign is probably the epitome of Installation Ceremonial. It is but natural, therefore, that the installation of the Master of a Lodge should be accompanied by an appropriate ceremonial – and so it is. In this paper it is hoped to give some brief account of the history of the Installation Ceremony and to remind all the brethren of the qualities to be looked for in the Master of a lodge.

It must be clearly understood that the Ceremony of Installed Master is *not*, under the Constitution of the Grand Lodge of Scotland, a masonic degree. There is no such thing as the 'Degree of Installed Master'. The Grand Lodge of Scotland recognises a Ceremonial of Installed Master and Law 85 states the conditions under which it may be conferred.

The Installed Master Ceremonial, as presently authorised by the Grand Lodge of Scotland, is not an indigenous part of Scottish freemasonry. This may come as a surprise to many, but the fact is that the ceremony was brought to Scotland from England in 1872 as the result of action on the part of Grand

Lodge. It is for that reason that an official ritual for the proper working of the ceremony is published.

In his *History of the Lodge of Edinburgh (Mary's Chapel) No 1*, Murray Lyon states that in the days of the operative lodges the installation into the principal office of the lodge was unmarked by any ceremonial other than the newly-elected brother taking an oath of fealty to the lodge and his brethren. The next step, again according to Murray Lyon, was the introduction of the dogma 'that no Brother could properly preside in a lodge until his reception of the Chair Degree'. Note that Murray Lyon uses the word 'degree'. This came about, says Murray Lyon, with the spread of the so-called 'High Degrees' at the end of the eighteenth and the beginning of the nineteenth centuries. This ceremony, which was termed variously 'Past Master', 'Master passed the Chair' and 'Scotch Past Master' was worked clandestinely in a number of Scottish Lodges and was an essential qualification for all who wished to become Royal Arch Masons in a Scottish Royal Arch Chapter. Indeed the Supreme Grand Royal Arch Chapter of Scotland authorised its conferring in their Chapters when the candidate had not attained it in his Lodge. It was abolished by the Supreme Grand Chapter of Scotland in 1887.

In 1858 the Grand Lodge of Scotland approved a form of Ceremonial for the 'Installation of the Chairman of a Lodge'. There is no mention in the minutes of Grand Lodge of any details of the actual ceremony employed. That some form of ritual was approved is certain, because at a conference between Grand Lodge and Grand Chapter, held on 20 April 1860, with reference to the Mark Degree, a joint recommendation was made 'as to the Past Master's Degree – that the Chairman of a lodge be installed according to the ceremonial approved by Grand Lodge in 1858'.

On 30 April 1872 the Grand Lodge of Scotland decided to import into Scottish Craft Masonry an 'Installed Ceremonial for Masters or Certified Past Masters only, similar to that practised in England and Ireland'. It was decided at the same time that a start should be made by the selection by Grand Lodge of three or more Masters or Past Masters who should

THE INSTALLED MASTER

procure their Installation at the hands of three or more English or Irish Installed Masters according to the customs of these countries. Thereafter they were to adjust a ritual suitable to Scotland and themselves install three or more Masters or Past Masters in Glasgow, Aberdeen, Dundee, Perth, or any large town where the Brethren might desire it.

Among the brethren who went to England was Brother William Hay of Rabbit Hall, an architect in Edinburgh and a Past Master of Lodge St Andrew, No 48. On his return from England he transmitted his knowledge at a meeting held in Freemason's Hall on 30 August 1872. At that meeting there were present the Master of the Lodge of Holyrood House (St Luke), No 44; Past Masters from Lodge St Kentigern, No 429; the Rifle Lodge, No 405, Lodge Commercial, No 360; St Clair, No 362, and Lodge Journeyman Masons, No 8. These brethren were duly installed into the Chair of King Solomon in accordance with the ritual of the ceremony adopted by Grand Lodge. This ritual is still the only one officially recognised by Grand Lodge, although a number of variants have crept in over the course of years.

From what has been said in the preceding paragraphs it is clear that Grand Lodge, in 1872, made an innovation in freemasonry. What was the reason behind this very unusual step? The principal reason seems to have been the difficulties met with by Scottish Masters and Past Masters when attending Installation meetings of English and Irish lodges. Not having passed through the Ceremony of an Installed Master, they had to retire during the actual installation and during what is known as the 'inner working'. Within the confines of the British Isles, this disadvantage was not perhaps of very great moment but it was important overseas. It is often almost impossible, in an overseas lodge, to get three Past Masters of the lodge at a meeting at the same time. This is due to the nature of Government and Commercial work, involving the frequent, and often sudden, transfer of a brother from one centre to another. Past Masters of Scottish lodges were unable to help their English or Irish brethren for they had not been installed. It now became possible for a Scottish Past Master to assist at the installation of an English or Irish Master, if he were called upon.

With the introduction of an officially approved Ceremonial for the Installation of a Master of a lodge, the old clandestine 'Passed Master' fell into desuetude and was no longer worked. A very similar, but not quite identical, ceremonial ultimately became the Installed Mark Master Degree under the Grand Lodge of Mark Master Masons of England. Of the variants in current use in Scotland, the principal one is in the opening of the Board of Installed Masters. In the official ceremonial the opening is accomplished by the Installing Master calling all present to order and opening the Board 'by declaration'. As a variant the Board of Installed Masters is opened at length – with question and answer – as if it were a degree and the Master Elect is *not* present at the opening. It is not possible to make further detailed comments here, but this variant might well be a carry-over from the opening of the old 'Passed Master Degree'. It seems possible that lodges which were working it continued to do so, but substituted the new inner working while retaining the old opening and closing.

While the Ceremony of the Installed Master is not peculiar to the three British Grand Lodges, it must not be assumed by Masters and Past Masters that all brethren who have occupied the chair of a lodge are, *ipso facto*, Installed Masters. The majority of the American Grand Lodges *do not* recognise any ceremony or degree of Installed Master. Visiting Masters and Past Masters from United States Grand Lodges must always be examined in detail as to their qualification to be present at a Board of Installed Masters. In the case of brethren from the Grand Lodges of Canada, Australia and New Zealand, no trouble will arise – these Grand lodges use the same Installation Ceremony as the British Grand Lodges – and this is also true of the Grand Lodge of India. Visitors from the Grand Lodges of Norway, Sweden, Denmark, Iceland, Holland, Germany, Austria and Switzerland are a special case and Grand Secretary should always be consulted if they desire to attend a Board of Installed Masters. The National Grand Lodge of France, which Scotland recognises, works the same ceremony as Scotland and their brethren may be admitted on proof.

To occupy the Chair of a lodge is undoubtedly to fill the highest office to which one's brethren can elect you. But the office is one which demands and should get the highest degree of leadership from he who fills it. It is perhaps pertinent to take a long and thoughtful look at the names of the men who served our lodges as Master a hundred, or even fifty years ago. Consider the positions of importance within the community that these men occupied, and then ask ourselves if our Masters today are of that quality. Very many are, and the Scottish Craft would be a poor thing if that were not so, but all too many lodges elect the Master as his reward for filling the junior offices – regardless of his abilities as a leader. The Constitutions of the Grand Lodge of Scotland do not require that a Master shall have first served the office of Warden (as many other Grand Lodges do). The members of a Scottish lodge are free to elect any qualified brother as their Master and there have been many good Masters elected 'straight from the floor'.

A Master is expected to be *Master* of his lodge, not someone to be pushed around. Theoretically he 'sets the lodge to work and gives good and wholesome instruction'. Yet what do we require for election as Master? There are no minimum requirements as to ritualistic proficiency; nothing with regard to the history, symbolism, ethics, law, philosophy and traditions of our Craft. We elect a Master and expect him somehow to be a leader. It rarely occurs to us to require some evidence – even from an outside source – of potential leadership.

There is far more to being a Master of a lodge than the mere recitation of the ritual. Some large lodges are paying the penalty of years of 'mass production'. When Masters of lodges are so lacking in imagination, knowledge and vision that they cannot conceive of a masonic meeting unless a degree is to be conferred, then we need not expect to admit and retain as useful members of the Craft, the real leaders in our various communities – be they village, burgh or city. The real Master of his lodge is he who can provide real leadership, a man who can give 'good and wholesome instruction', a man who understands what freemasonry is all about – even if he could not confer a single degree. Suppose he cannot recite the ritual? There are always those who are willing and anxious to do this work – and who can do it superbly. Let them have the charge of the lodge's ritualistic work – and let the Master 'rule and govern his lodge'. Scotland, along with the Scandinavian Grand Lodges, allows the Master to remain in office as long as his brethren care to elect him. This salutary arrangement is no longer exercised to the extent that it once was. One hundred years ago it was not uncommon for a Master to occupy the chair for seven or even ten years. The lodges appreciated a good Master, and when they got one – they kept him. There is much to be said for this idea and much less to be said for electing a Master as a reward for winning an endurance test.

3
THE DUKES OF ATHOLL AND FREEMASONRY

W. G. Fisher

THERE ARE MANY cases of families with a history of several generations taking part in freemasonry. Apart from our own Royal family, however, there can be few which have such a record as the Dukes of Atholl (also spelt Athole and Athol).

The family name was Murray and the Murrays and their retainers were Highlanders from Perthshire with a history of mixed loyalties. The first Duke was the 29th Earl and second Marquess of Atholl, Earl of Tullibardine. He was the eldest son and heir of John Murray, who was created Marquess of Atholl, on 17 February 1676. The first Duke's mother was Amelia Sophia, daughter and sole heir of James Stanley, Earl of Derby, through whom her grandson, the 2nd Duke succeeded to the sovereignty of the Isle of Man and the English Barony of Strange, created by writ in 1628. So far as we know, the first Duke was not a freemason in the English masonic system or a 'Gentleman Mason' in a Scots operative lodge. He was blind in one eye and was known as Iain Cam. He was a faithful supporter of William III, who, in 1696, conferred on him the titles of Earl of Tullibardine, Viscount Glenalmond and Lord Murray. This was in his father's lifetime and the titles became extinct when Iain Cam died. On 6 May 1703, he succeeded his father as Marquess of Atholl and on 30 June in the same year he was created Duke of Atholl, Marquess of Tullibardine, Earl of Strathtay and Strathardle, Viscount of

Balquhidder, Glenalmond and Glenlyon and Lord Murray, Balvenie and Gask, all in the County of Perth. Appointed Lord Privy Seal for Scotland in April 1703, he had previously been installed Knight of the Order of the Thistle, 7 February 1703/4. In the following year he surrendered his office of Lord Privy Seal and actively opposed the Union of Scotland with England. His second, but eldest surviving son, William, styled Marquess of Tullibardine, having joined the Earl of Mar in the 1715 Rebellion, was attainted by the United Kingdom Parliament and by law could not succeed to his father's titles and estates. The first Duke therefore procured an Act of Parliament vesting the succession in his next surviving son, James. When the first Duke died on 14 November 1724, the Jacobites styled the attainted Marquess of Tullibardine as 'Duke of Atholl'.

James Murray, 2nd Duke of Atholl

Lord James Murray, born 28 September 1690, at Edinburgh, third but 2nd surviving son, was a Captain and Lieutenant-Colonel of a Grenadier Company of the 1st Regt of Foot Guards in 1712 and was later Lieut-Colonel of the 1st Royal Scots Regiment of Foot. He was also MP for the County of Perth from 1715 to 1724. Lord James Murray married, first, Jane, widow of James Lannoy, of Hammersmith, a merchant, and daughter of Thomas Frederick, by whom he had two sons and two daughters. The two sons died in infancy. The elder daughter, Jean, married John Lindsay, 20th Earl of Crawford (Grand Master of England, 1734–35). The younger daughter, Charlotte, married her cousin, John, who became the 3rd Duke of Atholl. There was no issue of the second marriage. The Duke's second wife was Jean, daughter of John Drummond, of Megginch, Co. Perth.

No doubt the 2nd Duke foresaw some difficulties in regard to the succession, for in 1733 he obtained an Act of Parliament which provided that the attainder of his brother, the Marquess of Tullibardine, so far as it affected the honours and estates of the Dukes of Atholl, should apply only to that brother and his issue and not to any other heirs male of the first Duke. This brought into the succession the issue of his next surviving brother, Lord George Murray, who was pardoned for his part in the '15 Rebellion, but later was again to take up arms in the '45 Rebellion and end his days in exile. There was another brother, Lord Charles Murray, who was concerned in the '15 Rebellion. He was captured and sentenced to be shot as he had been an officer in the Army of the United Kingdom. His brother, the 2nd Duke, obtained a pardon for him, but he died in 1720. He and his brother, Lord George, were the most popular officers in the Jacobite Army.

We do not know when or where the 2nd Duke was made a Mason; he could have been a 'Gentleman Mason' in some Scottish operative lodge or he may have been initiated in an English lodge during one of his frequent visits to London, carrying out the duties of his public offices. We know that he was a freemason, because he attended the meeting of the Grand Lodge of England on 17 April 1735. The following is an extract from the minutes of that meeting:

> Thursday April 17th. 1735.
> At the House of the Rt. Honble. The Lord Viscount Weymouth, in Grosvenor Square where mett
> The Rt. Honble. The Earl of Craufurd G.M.
> Sr. Cecil Wray, Bart. D.G.M.
> John Ward Esqr. ⎱ G. Wardens
> Sr. Edward Mansell, Bart. ⎰
> The Rt. Honble. The Lord Viscount Weymouth G.M. Elect
> Duke of Richmond
> Duke of Athol
> Earl of Winchelsea
> Earl of Balcarrass (*Balcarres*)
> Earl of Wymes (*Wemyss, James, 5th Earl*)
> Earl of Lowdown (*Loudon*)
> Marquess of Bowman
> Lord Cathcart
> Lord Vere Bartee. (*Bertie*)

It will be noted that there were several other Scottish Peers present at this meeting. The Grand Lodge of Scotland was formed in the following year, but the Duke did not take any part in this, nor does he appear to have been considered for the Grand Mastership.

A Duke of Atholl is named in connection with an alleged meeting of Knights Templar in 1745 at Holyrood Palace, Edinburgh, when Prince Charles Edward is said to have been installed as Grand Master. The Duke referred to in the story must have been the Marquess of Tullibardine. The story, the truth of which is extremely doubtful, is told in *AQC* xxxiii, pp 40–45, and lxvii, pp 53–55, and need not be repeated here. It is fairly certain that the 2nd Duke of Atholl could not have been at Holyrood at the time stated.

During the '45 Rebellion he was in London, and his seat, Castle Blair, was seized by his brothers, William, Marquess of Tullibardine and Lord George Murray. He accompanied the Duke of Cumberland to Scotland, but he does not appear to have been in command of any troops.

He was a subscriber to Alexander Gordon's *Itinerarium Septentrionale* which was published in 1726, but this support of Alexander Gordon was probably not because Gordon was a freemason, but because the *Itinerarium* contained much useful information about ancient remains in Scotland.

The 2nd Duke of Atholl in 1736 succeeded his cousin, James Stanley, 10th Earl of Derby, in the sovereignty of the Isle of Man. The Duke is reported to have immediately appointed his nephew, James Murray (afterwards General James Murray) as Governor of the small kingdom, as it then was. If this is correct, James Murray must have been only fourteen years of age. The Duke himself visited the Island in 1739 and it was recorded at the time as follows:

> The Duke of Atholl was receiv'd as King in Man, by the Inhabitants of that Island with great Expressions of Joy. The firing of the great Guns was heard distinctly on the Coast of Galway.

At the same time he succeeded to the English Barony of Strange. Consequently, for four years he was both a representative Peer of Scotland and an English Peer, sitting in the House of Lords. He ceased to be a Scottish representative peer at the General election in 1741. He was Lord Privy Seal (Scotland) from 1733 to 1763, when he was appointed Keeper of the Great Seal and was installed Knight of the most Ancient and most Noble Order of the Thistle on 11 February 1733/34.

He died full of years at Dunkeld, Co. Perth, on 8 January 1764.

His portrait was engraved by Brother John Faber the younger (1695?–1756).

John Murray, 3rd Duke of Atholl

John Murray, who succeeded his uncle as 3rd Duke, was the son and heir of the 5th son of the first Duke, namely, Lord George Murray, who was the Lieut-General of the Jacobite Army in 1745. This Lord George Murray was exceedingly popular with his troops and a most able General. He was by far the best officer on the side of the Young Pretender. If his advice had been accepted the Battle of Culloden would have been avoided. His eldest brother, William, Marquess of Tullibardine, was a very sick man in 1745 and had to be supported by two servants whenever he stood up. He was eventually taken prisoner and died 9 July 1746, while he was prisoner in the Tower of London.

Lord George Murray, though wounded at Culloden, managed to escape to the Continent and he finally settled in Holland, where he died, 15 October 1760. His son, John, probably returned to Scotland while his father was still living in exile, for he is described as the Hon John Murray of Strowan. His maternal grandfather was James Murray of Glencarse and Strowan. John was born 6 May 1729, and became a Captain in Lord Loudon's Regiment of Foot, which later became the 54th (Highland) Regt. of Foot. He was MP for Co. Perth, 1761–64.

As there was some doubt whether he was entitled to succeed to the Dukedom of Atholl and the Atholl estates, he presented a petition to the King, claiming them and asking that a declaration be made that he was entitled to the same. The petition was referred to the House of Lords, who, on 7 February 1764, resolved 'that the Petitioner hath a right to the titles, honours and dignities of Duke of Atholl, Marquess of

Tullibardine, Earl of Strathay [sic] and Strathardle, Viscount Balquhidar, Glenalmond and Glenlyon, Lord Murray, Balvenie and Gask.'

On 23 October 1753, he married his cousin, Lady Charlotte Murray, only surviving daughter of the 2nd Duke. As the 2nd Duke's sole heir she became, on his death, the *suo jure* Baroness Strange and succeeded to the sovereignty and revenues of the Isle of Man. She and her husband in 1765 sold the sovereignty to the Government for £70,000 and a joint annuity of £2,000, reserving, however, their landed interests on the Island.

There appears to be no record of the lodge in which the Duke was made a Mason or the date when he was initiated. The Antients Grand Lodge in England, from its beginning, had some difficulty in persuading a Noble Freemason to be their Grand Master. The first was William, 1st Earl of Blesington, who had been Grand Master in Ireland some twenty years before. He was appointed Grand Master of the Antient Grand Lodge in 1756 and could be called the reluctant Grand Master. He was installed as Grand Master by proxy and during the three years he held the office he did not once attend a meeting of his Grand Lodge. All he seems to have done was to sign Warrants. He was followed as Grand Master by the 6th Earl of Kellie (1760 to 1765) and the Hon. Thomas Mathew (1766 to 1770).

The 3rd Duke of Atholl was elected Grand Master on 30 January and was installed 2 March 1771, at the Half Moon Tavern, in Cheapside. He appointed Laurence Dermott as his Deputy. For nearly twenty years Dermott had been Grand Secretary.

It was probably the third Duke who promoted the friendly relations which existed for many years between the Antients and the Grand Lodge of Scotland, especially when he was elected Grand Master Mason of Scotland on 20 November 1772, and installed as such a year later. He was a man of great character and charm and was noted for his generosity. In a letter dated 7 September 1774, he expressed his satisfaction that 'the Ancient Craft is regaining its ground over the

Moderns'. Two months later (5 November) he drowned himself in the River Tay at Dunkeld 'in a fit of delirium'. He was only forty-five years of age.

His widow, Charlotte, died 13 October 1805. They were buried at Dunkeld.

John Murray, 4th Duke of Atholl

John Murray, the 4th Duke, was the eldest son and heir of the 3rd Duke and was born on 30 June 1755, at Dunkeld. On the death of his mother he succeeded to the Barony of Strange and the Lordship of the Isle of Man. He presented his family's third petition to Parliament praying for a Bill to amend the Act of 1765, by which the sovereignty of the Isle of Man was sold to the British Crown, on the grounds that its terms were unjust. The two previous petitions had been dismissed. In spite of great opposition the Bill was brought in and passed. As a result of this, one-fourth of the customs of the Isle of Man was settled on him and the heirs general of the 7th Earl of Derby. In the year 1828, however, he commuted this for the sum of £417,000. He does not appear to have made his mark in any public offices, but in 1778 he raised a Regiment of two Battalions named the 77th Regiment of Foot, or Atholl Highlanders. The *Gentleman's Magazine* reported it as follows:

> The young Duke of Athole [*sic*] is raising a regiment of the same number (1,000 men) on his estate, in which he does not even ask a command. Besides the King's bounty-money, he gives two guineas to each recruit, which is 2,000 guineas out of his pocket. But, tempering zeal for his country with humanity to his countrymen, he obliges himself to maintain the families of the recruits who go from his estate, if they need maintenance, and never, during his life, to raise the rents upon the families of such tenants as resort to his standard.

The minutes of the Lodge of Kelso, No 58 (SC), contain the following reference to the same matter:

> A special meeting of the Lodge was held on February 12, 1778, when the Right Worshipful explained that Lieut.-Colonel Brown of the Swan in Chelsea, of the Athol Highlanders, being in town and levying men for the corps raising by the Most Worshipful the

Duke of Athol, Grand Master of England and Grand Master Elect of Scotland.

The brethren unanimously resolved to testify their zeal for their sovereign and their respect for the Noble Grand Master by marching with Lieut.-Colonel Brown at the head of his recruiting party beating up for volunteers for the Athol Highlanders, and accordingly marched from the Lodge in Procession through the town and at the same time offered a Bounty of Three Guineas over his Majesty's allowance to every man who should enlist in that Corps.

There had previously been a 77th Regiment of Foot, named the Montgomery Highlanders, which was raised in 1757 and disbanded in 1763. The Atholl Highlanders were disbanded at Berwick on Tweed in 1783. Most of the time it was embodied the Regiment was in Ireland. On 5 October 1783, the Grand Lodge of Ireland granted Warrant No 578 for the establishment of a Lodge in the Regiment. The Duke of Atholl had just completed his year as Grand Master of Scotland and was still Grand Master of the Antients in England!

Presumably, it was for raising the Atholl Highlanders that the Duke was created, 18 August 1786, as Baron Murray of Stanley, Co. Gloucester, and Earl Strange. This enabled him to sit in the House of Lords as an English Peer, during his mother's lifetime; since 1780 he had been a Representative Peer for Scotland. Other offices and appointments which he held were:

1780	Fellow of the Royal Society.
1793	(4th February) Captain General and Commander in Chief of the Isle of Man.
1794–1803	Lord Lieutenant of the county of Perth.
1797	(28th June) Privy Councillor.
1798	Colonel of the Perthshire Militia.
1800	Knight of the Most Ancient and Most Noble Order of the Thistle.

The 4th Duke was not a mason when his father died and the Antient Grand Lodge, either desperately anxious to maintain the Atholl connection, or remembering the difficulty they always had in persuading a noble freemason to be their Grand

Master, prevailed upon him to succeed his father as their Grand Master. In order to make this possible, although he was only nineteen years of age, he was initiated, passed, raised and installed Master of the Grand Master's Lodge No 1, all on 25 February, 1775. I do not have to point out that this was the Grand Lodge which had accused the older Grand Lodge of violating the ancient Landmarks of the Order. Four months later, on 25 June, he was installed as Grand Master, in the presence of the Duke of Leinster and Sir James Adolphus Oughton, Past Grand Masters of Ireland and Scotland respectively.

It is owing to his great influence and the services he rendered to the Antients that they became known as Atholl Masons and Antient Lodges as Atholl Lodges.

It is a question whether he took more than a passing interest in freemasonry at this early age. He was little more than a boy, but master of something like 200,000 acres and a most eligible bachelor. The Antients had been dominated almost from the beginning of their Grand Lodge by Laurence Dermott who did not rule with velvet gloves and some of the things he did was not always above reproach. Indeed, he had to defend himself and his autocratic behaviour in 1778. In the 3rd Edition of *Ahiman Rezon* he wrote

> . . . some of the Modern society have been extremely malapert of late. Not satisfied with saying the Antient Masons in England had no Grand Master, some of them descended so far from the truth as to report the author [ie *Dermott*] had forged the Grand Master's handwriting to masonical Warrants, &c. Upon application, his Grace the Most Noble Prince John, Duke of Atholl, our present Right Worshipful Grand Master, avowed his Grace's handwriting, supported the ancient Craft and vindicated the author in public newspapers.

This would have carried more weight if he had produced facsimiles of the disputed signatures. It would also have been interesting to know in which papers this vindication appeared. The newspapers of the period have been well scanned for masonic information but this acquittal of Dermott has still to come to light. The Duke, of course, in the circumstances, would scarcely refuse to support his Deputy, the mainspring of the Antient's organisation.

It is impossible to say if there was any real friction between the Duke and Dermott, but the former does not appear to have attended many meetings during this first period of office as Grand Master of the Antients. About the end of 1777 Dermott resigned his office of Deputy Grand Master. The Duke expressed in a letter his approval of William Dickey as Deputy Grand Master and at the same time informed the Grand Lodge that he had accepted the office of Grand Master Mason of Scotland, 'as he imagined it might accrue to the advantage of Antient Masonry in England by indubitably showing the tenets to be the same'. He is recorded in the *Year Book of the Grand Lodge of Scotland* as 'Grand Master Mason. 1778–80'.

The Duke declined re-election as Grand Master of the Antients in a letter in 1781, of which the following is a copy:

> Dunkeld, Nov. 29. 1781.
> Right Worshipful Grand Secretary,
>
> I had the honour of receiving a copy of the Proceedings of the Grand Lodge on the 5th of Sep. and your letter yesterday.
>
> I should accept with the greatest pleasure of the honor the Grand Lodge have done me by re-electing me their Grand Master; but as my Residence is chiefly in the Country it has not been (nor will it I fear be) in my power to give that attendance which is the due of the Ancient Freaternity. I trust that during the time I have had the honor of being Grand Master, the Honor and Interest of the Craft have no way diminished, but for the reason above mentioned, with many thanks to the Grand Lodge I must beg leave to resign the high office of Grand Master, at the same time the Fraternity may rest assured of my best wishes for their welfare, and the Prosperity of the Ancient Craft.
>
>   I remain,
>   Right Worshipful Grand Secretary,
>   Your faithful Br. in Masonry,
>   (Signed) ATHOLL, Grand Master.

In 1791, Laurence Dermott died. For forty-seven years he had ruled the Grand Lodge of England 'Under the old Institutions', admired by many, supported in the end by few, execrated by some. In the same year, the Marquess of Antrim, who had succeeded the Duke of Atholl as Grand Master, also died. The Duke once more accepted nomination as Head of the Antients and was unanimously elected and on 20 January 1792, installed as their Grand Master. There is no doubt that it was a very popular appointment.

During this second period of office as Grand Master the Duke showed himself to be a zealous, courageous and enlightened leader. He was no longer a figurehead, though much of the administration of his Grand Lodge had necessarily to be left to his Deputies, James Agar (1790–94); William Dickey (1794–1800); and Thomas Harper (1801–13). It was largely due to his enthusiastic influence that the Boys' School was established in 1798. In *Ahiman Rezon* (7th Edition) he alone is credited with the introduction of a clause in the Secret Societies Act of 1799, which exempted freemasons' lodges from the Provisions of the Act. It was, of course, the result of the united efforts of the Duke and the Earl of Moira, Acting Grand Master of the Moderns.

This association with the Earl of Moira lasted many years and was an important factor in the events which led to the Union of the two Grand Lodges in 1813. It also brought about the fraternal recognition by the Grand Lodge of Scotland of the Moderns Grand Lodge of England.

The Union of the two Grand Lodges in England in 1813 has been recorded at some length by competent masonic writers, but the story of the bitter opposition he had to overcome in his own Grand Lodge has yet to be told in full. It is a subject which requires more space than is available here. One must state, however, that in order to facilitate matters the Duke of Atholl resigned as Grand Master of the Antients on the day of the Feast of the four Crowned Martyrs, 8 November 1813. In his place his Royal Highness the Duke of Kent was installed as Grand Master on 1 December, the same day on which the Articles of Union were ratified. His brother, the Duke of Sussex, Grand Master of the Moderns, then became the Grand Master of the United Grand Lodge of England.

The Duke of Atholl continued to take an active interest in

Freemasonry. He was First Grand Principal of the RA in Scotland from 1820 till his death in 1830. About the year 1822 he agreed to preside over the Rite of Misraim, an unrecognised masonic rite of 90 Degrees, said to have originated in Milan about 1805. The Sovereign of the Rite in England was HRH the Duke of Sussex, and in Ireland, the Duke of Leinster. After the Union he also became one of four Vice-Patrons of the Girls' School.

He married, first, 26 December 1774, Jane, eldest daughter of Charles, 9th Lord Cathcart. She died in Hanover Square, London, 5 December 1790, aged 37 years, and was buried at Dunkeld. He married, secondly, 11 March 1794, Margery, widow of John Mackenzie (styled Lord Macleod) and eldest daugher of James, 16th Lord Forbes.

The Duke died at Dunkeld 29 September 1830 aged seventy-five years and was buried beside his first wife.

John Murray, 5th Duke of Atholl
Born 26 June 1778, the 5th Duke lived under most tragic circumstances. Educated at Eton he was appointed an Ensign in the 61st Foot (South Gloucestershire Regt.) in 1797. In the following year he became mentally ill and for the rest of his life required care and protection. He died in Greville Place, St John's Wood, Middlesex, 14 September 1846. He was not a freemason.

George Augustus Frederick John Murray, 6th Duke of Atholl
The father of the 6th Duke was James Murray, created Lord Glenlyon, 9 July 1821, 2nd son of the 4th Duke by his first wife. This James Murray married Emily Francis, daughter and in her issue sole heir of Hugh Percy, 2nd Duke of Northumberland.

The 6th Duke of Atholl was born 20 September 1814, in London. At about the age of 20 years he received a Commission in the 2nd Dragoon Guards. In 1840 he resigned from the Army perhaps because three years before he had succeeded his father as Lord Glenlyon. He was a Lord in Waiting from January to July 1846, and was installed a Knight of the Thistle, 28 October 1853. He was also President of the

Highland and Agricultural Society from 1858 to 1862, and hereditary Sheriff of the County of Perth.

He rendered most distinguished service to freemasonry in Scotland, almost from the day he was initiated in the Dunkeld Lodge, No 14 (SC) in November 1841. On the last day of that month (St Andrew's Day) he was appointed Depute Grand Master by Major-General Lord Frederick Fitz-Clarence, who was installed Grand Master Mason on that date. Lord Glenlyon was re-elected Depute Grand Master on St Andrew's Day in the following year. After the meeting of Grand Lodge on that day, he took the chair at the dinner which followed and we are told:

> His Lordship did the honours of the chair in excellent style and exerted himself to the utmost in keeping up the good feeling and conviviality of the meeting.

On 8 May 1843, he attended the funeral Grand Lodge held by the Grand Master Mason of Scotland in commemoration of the Duke of Sussex, Grand Master of the United Grand Lodge of England, who had died on 21 April in that year.

On St Andrew's Day, 1843, he was elected Grand Master Mason of Scotland. He held this office for 21 years, much longer than any other GMM of Scotland. All that time he worked with unflagging zeal for the improvement of Scottish Freemasonry. He also held the supreme office in other degrees. For example, he was installed a Knight Templar in the Lothians Preceptory on 29 November 1843, and on the following 11 March he was appointed Chancellor of the Order of the Temple and was Grand Master of the Order from 1846 to 1864. Exalted in the Royal Arch Chapter No 1, Edinburgh, in 1843, he was First Grand Principal, 1844–46, and also from 1847 to 1850. After the meeting of Chapter No 1, on 23 September 1844, the First Principal said:

> The Companions will, I am sure, join with great pleasure in dedicating a bumper to the health of her most gracious majesty, the Queen and the more so as on the present occasion she was the guest of our Most Excellent First Principal of the Supreme Grand Royal Arch Chapter of Scotland, Companion Lord Glenlyon, who

was during the last twelve months exalted in this Chapter. Her Majesty's confidence was unbounded, having dismissed her guards and trusted to the far-famed hospitality and loyalty of the Atholl Highlanders for protection.

The Atholl Highlanders at that time were the bodyguard of the Dukes of Atholl and it was about this time that Queen Victoria gave her royal assent to the maintenance of this private army. It is the only private army permitted in the United Kingdom.

On 14 September 1846, he succeeded his Uncle as 6th Duke of Atholl, or, as he spelt the name from about 1847, Athole. In order to be consistent we will continue to use the word Atholl especially as this was restored by his son and successor.

In the early days of his Grand Mastership he realised the value of visiting the lodges under his jurisdiction. As Depute Grand Master he visited St Mary's Chapel, Edinburgh, on 29 November 1842, accompanied by several office bearers of Grand Lodge. He visited the lodge again in 1847 when he was Grand Master Mason.

For more than one hundred years a Grand Master Mason of Scotland had not visited Glasgow. This was remedied on 1 June 1847, when the Duke attended a meeting in the Great Hall at the Trades Hall, Glasgow, for the purpose of installing Sheriff Alison as Prov Grand Master of Glasgow. Sheriff Alison was Archibald Alison (afterwards Sir Archibald) the author of *The History of Europe* and *The Life of John, Duke of Marlborough*. The Duke visited Glasgow again on 27 February 1851, to attend the annual Masonic Ball and on 9 April to lay the foundation stone of Victoria Bridge, which replaced one which had withstood corroding time for 500 years. On 12 December, the same year, he visited the Prov Grand Lodge of Aberdeen, the first GMM to do so.

Many difficulties arose during the time he was Grand Master Mason of Scotland, but he showed considerable firmness and tact in dealing with them. The facilities provided by masonic clubs in Edinburgh and Glasgow was abused by brethren as well as by visitors who were not all masons. They caused so much scandal that the civil authorities and Grand Lodge had to intervene. Then there was the rather strained relations with

English Freemasons following some tactless remarks by Dr Crucefix regarding some Scottish Freemasons, who, he claimed, came into England, claiming relief from funds intended for English Freemasons and their dependants. In 1850 an attempt was made to elect someone else as Grand Master. The incident led to tumult and disorder in Grand Lodge. The Duke dealt with the matter calmly and judiciously and in the end was re-elected by an overwhelming majority.

He was very jealous of what he considered to be the ancient rights and privileges of Scottish Masons. Bro D. Murray Lyon tells the story of a brush the Duke had with the Prince Consort:

> . . . When in 1851 Prince Albert was invited to lay the foundation stone of the Fine Arts Gallery in Edinburgh, his Grace failing to persuade his Royal Highness to join the Order, declined under protest to countenance the proceedings. Again, in 1861, when made aware of the Prince Consort's intention to plant the corner-stones of the new Post Office and Industrial Museum at Edinburgh, his Grace addressed a letter to his Royal Highness, in which he said: 'I consider it my duty, as Grand Master Mason of Scotland, again respectfully to protest against the infringement of the ancient privilege of the Masonic Bodies to lay the foundation-stones of public buildings in Scotland'. The Prince replied that he had made enquiry and found that Freemasons possessed no such exclusive right as had been claimed by his Grace.

This, however, did not diminish the high regard Queen Victoria had for him and she visited him during his last illness.

The Empress Eugenie of France and her husband also treated him with great respect. When on a visit to the Emperor Napoleon III in the autumn of 1861, the Duke was not expected back in time to preside over his Grand Lodge on St Andrew's Day. Arrangements had been made for the Depute Grand MM to take his place when, to the surprise of the Grand Officers, he arrived in time to carry out his duties at the Festival.

The Grand Lodge of Scotland had never possessed a place of its own, its meetings being held in various halls in Edinburgh. In 1856, however, a sum of £3,500 was voted for the purchase of a house in George Street, Edinburgh, with the intention of building on the site, a permanent home for Grand Lodge. The ceremony of laying the foundation stone was conducted by the Duke of Atholl on 24 June 1858. The new hall was consecrated by him on 24 February 1859, and since that time Freemasons' Hall in George Street, Edinburgh, has been the headquarters of the Grand Lodge of Scotland.

The Duke was married 29 October 1839, at Blair Drummond, to Anne, only daughter of Henry Home-Drummond. She was born 17 June 1814, in Edinburgh. From February to December 1852, she was Mistress of the Robes and was a Lady of the Bedchamber from 1854 to 1897. She died at Dunkeld, 18 May 1897, having outlived the Duke for 33 years. He died of a cancer in the neck at Blair Castle, 16 January 1864. A Funeral Grand Lodge was held in his honour and a dirge was composed for that occasion by the Grand Bard, James Ballantine. In 1865 a Celtic Cross was erected to his memory by masonic friends on Logieriat Hill, overlooking the Vale of Atholl.

John James Hugh Henry Stewart-Murray, 7th Duke of Atholl

His Grace was the only son and heir of the 6th Duke and was born at Blair Castle on 6 August 1840.

He was introduced to freemasonry at an early age for when in 1856 his father invited upwards of 100 brethren from Dundee to visit him at Blair Castle, some of them were shown round the grounds by the young Marquess of Tullibardine. He was only 18 years of age when he was initiated in the Lodge of St John, No 14, Dunkeld (now the United Lodge of Dunkeld) on St Andrew's Day, 1858. On the same day he was taken to Edinburgh to attend Grand Lodge, which was held on that day to re-elect his father as Grand Master Mason. The Marquess was passed in the Dunkeld Lodge on 12 January 1859, but four years were to elapse before he was raised and then it was far from the place where he first saw the light. He was raised on 24 March 1863, in St Paul's Lodge, No 374, Montreal, which still works under the jurisdiction of the Grand Lodge of England.

This delay in being raised to the degree of MM may indicate a lack of that enthusiasm which had characterised previous members of his family who had distinguished themselves in freemasonry. He was, however, Senior Grand Warden of Scotland from 1866–68 and Provincial Grand Master for Perthshire West, from 1864 to 1886.

In 1859 the Marquess obtained a Lieutenantcy in the Scots Fusilier Guards and was a Captain from 1864 to 1866. Through his grandmother he succeeded to the Barony of Percy when his great-uncle, Algernon Percy, 4th Duke of Northumberland, died on 12 February, 1865.

On his father's death he became 7th Duke of Atholl and on 1 December 1865, he registered at the Lyon Office, Edinburgh, the assumption of the name of Stewart before that of Murray. This was in consideration of his descent from and representation of the Stewarts, Earls of Atholl. He was installed Knight of the Thistle, 14 May 1868.

On 29 October 1863, he married Louisa, eldest daughter of Sir Thomas Moncrieffe, of Moncrieffe. She died in Italy on 8 July 1902, and was buried at Blair. The Duke died on 20 January 1917, and was succeeded by his son, the Marquess of Tullibardine.

John George Stewart-Murray, 8th Duke of Atholl (b. 1871)
The 8th Duke revived faintly the masonic glories of his predecessors for as Marquess of Tullibardine he was Grand Master Mason of Scotland from 1909 to 1913.

He was initiated in the Dunkeld Lodge on 24 October, 1892, and was exalted in the RA Chapter No 40 in 1909 and installed in the Lothians KT Preceptory in 1920.

Before he succeeded as Duke of Atholl he had a distinguished career in the Army. He was a 2nd Lieutenant in the Royal Horse Guards in 1892 and was promoted Lieutenant in 1893, Captain, 1899, Brevet Major, 1900, and Lieut-Colonel in 1903. He served in the Sudan in 1893, being present at the Battle at Atbara and at the capture of Khartoum. He was mentioned in despatches and awarded the DSO (15 November 1898) and the British and Khedive's Medals. He also served in the South African War from 1899–1902 and was three times mentioned in despatches. He was called to further service during World War I and was again mentioned in despatches and was made a Companion of the Order of the Bath. He was awarded the White Eagle of Serbia, 3rd Class, with Swords. The many appointments he held from time to time included: Brig-General and Brigade Commander, HQ Unit (1918); Colonel Commandant, Scottish Horse; Hon Colonel, 10th Liverpool Regiment; Hon Colonel, 3rd Bn The Black Watch; Hon Brig-General (Retired) Territorial Army, 1927; President of the Perthshire Territorial Army Association. He was Lord Lieutenant of Perthshire and was installed Knight of the Thistle in 1918 and appointed to the Privy Council on 21 November 1921.

As Marquess of Tullibardine he was MP for West Perthshire from 1910 to 1917. Shortly after succeeding his father as 8th Duke of Atholl he was appointed Lord High Commissioner of the General Assembly of the Church of Scotland and received the Freedom of Edinburgh in 1928.

He married 20 July 1899, Katherine Margery, 4th daughter of Sir James Henry Ramsey, Bart, of Banff. She was a most distinguished lady in her own right and was MP for Kinross and West Perth from 1923–1938, and Parliamentary Secretary of the Board of Education 1924–29. She was made a Dame of the Order of the British Empire in 1918 and was Hon DCL, Oxon, Durham, McGill and Columbia (New York).

The Duke died on 16 March 1942, and the Duchess on 21 October 1960. They did not leave a son to succeed to the title and estates.

James Thomas Stewart-Murray, 9th Duke of Atholl

The 9th Duke was brother and heir-apparent of the 8th Duke. He was born 18 August, 1879, and like his brother chose the Army as a career. As a Major in the 1st Bn Cameron Highlanders he served in South Africa from 1900 to 1902. In World War I he was wounded in 1914 and was taken prisoner.

He was initiated in the Dunkeld Lodge, but was never advanced beyond the rank of Entered Apprentice. Consequently he made no progress in Freemasonry. He was inclined to be eccentric, for after succeeding to the Dukedom he always called himself Lord James Murray.

He died unmarried 8 May 1957.

George Iain Murray, 10th Duke of Atholl
The 10th Duke of Atholl was a distant cousin of his predecessor in the title, tracing his direct descent from the Right Revd Lord George Murray, Bishop of St Davids, 2nd son of the 3rd Duke.

His Grace, who is the present Duke of Atholl, is not a freemason.

(Reprinted with kind permission of Quatuor Coronati Lodge No 2076, London, from Volume 80 of the printed Transactions of the Lodge.)

4

ROBERT BURNS – FREEMASON

Fred J. Belford

AMONG THE GREAT men whose memories Scotsmen in particular have been delighted to perpetuate few, if any, have been held in greater love and admiration than Robert Burns, the national poet of Scotland. Indeed, the enthusiasm which is aroused as each succeeding January comes round is a source of continual wonder to other nations and it certainly has no parallel in any other country. In this article we shall deal mainly with Burns's activities as a freemason and as such Scotsmen should be immensely proud that the Bard was a member of the Fraternity. As we shall see, masonry and Scottish masonry at that, played no mean part in giving to the world the poetry of Robert Burns.

According to Dr Halliday, 'One prime factor which assisted to unite all classes in eighteenth-century Scotland into a recognised brotherhood, and provided the opportunity and sanction for voluntary co-operation, was the bond of Freemasonry; not Freemasonry as we know it today with all its modern trappings and symbolic teaching, but the earlier jolly Brotherhood with its gatherings at the local inn. There is no cause for wonder or surprise that in the fulness of time Robert Burns became a Freemason: the wonder would have been if he had not.' The heart of the poet was a soil ideal to the seeds of freemasonry, for the beautiful teaching of the Craft is alive with the very essence of poetry. His abiding interest in, and love of all that was in any way connected with the Order no doubt coloured much of his poetry and ultimately found expression in 'A man's a man for a' that', the great poem on the Brotherhood of Man. In that poem, and especially in the last verse, we find expressed the whole of the grand ideal of freemasonry. This is not to say, however, that such a poem was wholly inspired by freemasonry, because Burns would have written in this vein had he never entered the door of a masonic lodge.

Masonry made a direct appeal to one of his temperament, loving as he did social companions, and who himself was the life and soul in any congenial company. Not only so, but freemasonry was flourishing so strongly in Tarbolton at the time that it was to be expected that in due course he would enter fervently into everything concerned with the Order. Freemasonry gave him an impetus, and we cannot doubt that the hours he spent with the brethren helped in no small way to lighten many a dark hour in his life and cheered him between his periods of despondency.

> The social, friendly, honest man
>   Whate'er he be,
> 'Tis he fulfils great Nature's plan
>   And none but he.

Another typically masonic verse by him is:

> A' ye whom social pleasure charms,
> Whose heart the tide of kindness warms,
> Wha hold your being on the terms
>   'Each aid the others,'
> Come to my bowl, come to my arms,
>   My friends, my brothers.

His enthusiasm for freemasonry was mainly attributable to his sociable disposition, and there is sufficient testimony that Burns was not given to conviviality merely to satisfy a craving for strong drink. But the influence of masonry on his life must be put into its proper perspective, for there is no denying that the part it played in the publication of his poems cannot be overlooked. It would appear to be manifestly unfair on the part of Carlyle and several other of his biographers that either not a word has come from their pen or, if it did, it was to depreciate his connection with the Craft. In fact, to omit or slight Burns's masonic career is surely unjust to him and to freemasonry. His association with the brethren indeed was a means of enabling him to meet persons of a higher social status than himself and of introducing him to families of distinction, especially during his stay in Edinburgh, and at the same time helping to raise him from obscurity to the place he so richly deserves – the national poet of Scotland.

During the fifteen years (1781–1796) which covered his masonic career he devoted himself wholeheartedly to all that pertained to the Brotherhood, making that 'daily advancement' of which our First Charge stresses the importance.

Burns's masonic life might conveniently be divided, like all Gaul, into three parts. The first part includes his initiation into the Fraternity and his active work in his native county of Ayr, the historic home of freemasonry. Included also in this period is the publication of the now famous and priceless Kilmarnock Edition of his poems. The second comprises the two periods he spent in Edinburgh, where masonry did not enter particularly prominently into his life, probably because of the assiduous attention he was giving to the publication of his Edinburgh Edition. The chief matter of interest in his visit to the capital is the controversy surrounding his supposed inauguration as Poet Laureate of Lodge Canongate Kilwinning. The third division concerns his declining years in Dumfriesshire, where he again resumed his masonic interests though, partly owing to illness, to a lesser extent.

In 1781 the Burns family tenanted the farm of Lochlea, near Tarbolton, having come there from Mount Oliphant in 1777. Robert, before joining the Craft, had attended a school in Kirkoswald in the practical use of instruments concerned with mensuration and surveying, the Square, the Level, etc., and so, at the beginning of his masonic career he was already well versed in the operative uses of a mason's working tools. He tells us that while in Kirkoswald he went on with a high hand at his geometry till the sun entered Virgo, which was always a carnival in his bosom.

The history of freemasonry round about the period with

which we are dealing was of a somewhat turbulent nature. On 17 May 1771, Lodge Tarbolton Kilwinning had received its Charter from Mother Kilwinning. Twenty of the brethren, seeing clearly that the power of the latter was on the decline, wished to erect a lodge under the jurisdiction of the Grand Lodge of Scotland which since 1736 was steadily growing in power and so St David's, Tarbolton, No 174, was chartered on 5 February 1773. Those who were left in the original Tarbolton Kilwinning Lodge also saw the wisdom of working under Grand Lodge and so they too applied for recognition. This resulted in 1774 in the erection of a new Lodge, St James's Tarbolton, No 178. The Grand Master Mason at the time was John, 3rd Duke of Athole. No doubt a little jealousy in this case crept in over the original secession. At the same time the brethren were fully aware that there was not room in such a small village as Tarbolton for two lodges. It was accordingly agreed to sink all differences and the two lodges combined on 25 June 1781, under the name of Lodge St David, Tarbolton, since this lodge held 'the oldest charter' from Grand Lodge, 'probably a compliment or concession', according to Chambers, 'designed to appease the schismatic body'.

Into this united lodge Burns, nine days after the union, was initiated in his twenty-third year, and his name recorded in the Minute Book as follows: 'Sederant for 4th July. Robert Burns in Lochly was entered an Apprentice, Joph. Norman M.' His initiation fee was 12s 6d, and was paid on the same day.

The lodge met in John Richard's public house where the Bachelors' Club, founded in 1780 by Burns and other kindred spirits, had a room. This house has been recently renovated and is now in an excellent state of repair. The following is from the preamble which Burns himself wrote regarding this club:

> Of birth or blood we do not boast,
> Nor gentry does our club afford;
> But ploughmen and mechanics we
> In nature's simple dress record.

The social urge and the opportunities he had for expressing his thoughts fluently there were very soon to bear fruit in his lodge.

Shortly after his initiation he removed to Irvine to learn flax-dressing. This upset for a time his masonic attendances, but on 1 October 1781, he was passed to the Fellowship Degree and raised to the Degree of Master as set forth in the brief Minute: 'Robert Burns in Lochly was passed and raised', signed by the Master, the Wardens, Secretary and Treasurer.

The united lodge enjoyed a brief history of only a few months, but a history rendered glorious for all time by having the peculiar distinction of making Burns a freemason. Nor did the union appear to have been a happy one. Apparently that harmony which should characterise masons the world over was lacking. At any rate, a fresh disruption took place the following year, June 1782. Burns was one of the seceders. Some of the members doubtless objected to Lodge St James losing its identity and it was to be expected that it was only a matter of time before a separate lodge would be formed. This materialised on 17 June 1782, under its former name of St James, Tarbolton. Some years later, a list of its members was sent in to Grand Lodge, and the names of these members are found engrossed in the books there. Burns's name does not appear in this list, possibly because only the names of intrants, after the lodge had become a separate body, were submitted to Grand Lodge. This is borne out by the fact that the name of Gilbert Burns, who was made a mason five years after the erection of St James's Lodge, appears only about a dozen names from the top. On the other hand, this neglect may have been occasioned by the carelessness of Grand Lodge officials at the time who have been alleged to have been very much averse to such dry labour as the enrolment of names. Lodge Tarbolton Kilwinning St James now appears on the Roll of the Grand Lodge of Scotland as No 135 and possesses a large commodious hall of its own in the centre of the village. Lodge St David became dormant in 1843, but was reponed in 1869 as No 133, with Mauchline as its meeting place. It has some interesting relics consisting of jewels, plate for printing diplomas of the lodge, Master's chair, chest, lodge glasses, toddy-ladles, and a minute book. These are now believed to be in safe custody in Ayr.

At a meeting of the Grand Lodge of Scotland in May 1951, it was reported that the minute books containing details of the initiation of Burns into freemasonry, now in private hands, were valued at £3,000. The Grand Librarian informed the Grand Committee that a lady in Kilmarnock had in her possession certain old minute books and other items lately belonging to Lodge St David, No 133. When the lodge became dormant in 1843 the Charter was recovered by the Provincial Grand Master and returned to Grand Lodge. The minute books passed into private hands. The lodge was reponed in 1869 and, although the Charter was returned, the minute books were not. In 1925 the law agent advised the Grand Committee that an action would have to be raised against the lady if it were decided to prove title. No action was taken.

Burns's name is not recorded in the minutes of St James's Lodge until 1784. But his keen interest in the lodge is evident from the following letter in his handwriting, but not necessarily composed by him, addressed to the Master, Sir John Whitefoord, Bart, of Ballochmyle, on behalf of the seceders in connection with the dispute towards the end of 1782:

> 'Sir, – We who subscribe to this are members of St James's Lodge, Tarbolton, and one of us is in the office of Warden, and as we have the honour of having you for Master of our Lodge, we hope you will excuse this freedom, as you are the proper person to whom we ought to apply. We look on our Mason Lodge to be a serious matter, both with respect to the character of Masonry itself, and likewise as it is a charitable society. This last, indeed, does not interest you farther than a benevolent heart is interested in the welfare of its fellow creatures; but to us, Sir, who are of the lower orders of mankind, to have a fund in view, on which we may with certainty depend to be kept from want should we be in circumstances of distress, or old age, that is a matter of high importance.
>
> We are sorry to observe that our Lodge's affairs, with respect to its finances, have for a good while been in a wretched condition. We have considerable sums in bills which lie by without being paid, or put in execution, and many of our members never mind their yearly dues, or anything else belonging to our Lodge. And since the separation from St David's we are not even sure of our

existence as a Lodge. There has been a dispute before the Grand Lodge, but how decided, or if decided at all, we know not.

For these and other reasons we humbly beg the favour of you, as soon as convenient, to call a meeting, and let us consider on some means to retrieve our wretched affairs.

We are, etc.'

On 30 June 1784 the famous Manson" Inn, the Cross Keys, became the meeting place, the proprietor being Treasurer to the lodge. This old inn is no longer in existence, but its locus has been indicated by a tablet placed in a corner of the garden. A month later, on 27 July, Burns was elected Depute Master, an office which was then elective and of much more practical importance than it is today. This position carried with it the active duties of a Master, who in these days was little more than a figurehead, and attended meetings but rarely. So Burns was in reality the virtual head of the Lodge, and it is on record that he carried through his work with marked ability. He held the Depute Mastership till St John's Day, 1788.

> Oft have I met your social band,
> And spent the cheerful festive night;
> Oft honour'd with supreme command,
> Presided o'er the Sons of Light.

His first minute as Depute Master, and which is wholly in his handwriting although unsigned, shows his keen interest in the lodge:

> This night the Lodge met and ordered four pounds of candles and one quire of eightpence paper for the use of the Lodge, which money was laid out by the Treasurer and the candles and paper laid in accordingly.

By his enthusiasm he justified his election to the leading place in the lodge. Robert Chambers tells us 'that according to the reports of old associates he was so keen a mason that he would hold lodges for the admission of new members in his own house', and it was at one of these that his brother Gilbert was admitted to the Craft.

He was himself most faithful in his attendance at lodge meetings. During 1785 he was present at nine meetings, and it was because of an incident at one of these where the 'vainglorious tendencies' of the village schoolmaster gave birth to his amusing poem, 'Death and Doctor Hornbook'. The story is so well known that there is no need to detail it here. The famous colloquy between himself and Death has been read by thousands with amusement and delight and has conferred an immortality on John Wilson, the dominie, which he scarcely deserved.

A quaint regulation dated 7 December 1785, written by John Wilson (Dr Hornbook) and signed 'Robert Burness' is worthy of mention at this point.

> The Lodge thought proper to writing that old regulation. That who ever stands as Master shall be bound at the entry of a new member for that members dues if the money is not paid or security such as the Lodge shall approve of.

In 1786 Burns again attended nine meetings, at the second of which, on 1 March, he passed and raised his brother Gilbert. It is interesting to note that he signed the minute of this meeting 'Robert Burns'. Up to this date he had used the signature 'Robert Burness'. Apparently during all this time, though living some miles from the village, he never missed a single meeting of his lodge and on several occasions, as we have seen, he held subordinate meetings in Mauchline, thus doing his utmost to promote the tenets of freemasonry.

For a time at least Gilbert Burns took an active part in the affairs of the lodge. His name appears in the minute book on five separate occasions between 11 December 1786 and 21 December 1787, and he occupied the Chair on two occasions, when the lodge met at Mauchline on 18 and 20 November 1788. In July 1787 he had a loan from the lodge of £6 5s (a not uncommon practice in those days), which he repaid in June 1788.

It soon became apparent that the brethren were not satisfied with their meeting place in Manson's Tavern, and they began to look around for more suitable quarters. We find a curious proposition recorded in the minute of 15 June:

> It was proposed by the Lodge that, as they much wanted a

Lodge-room, a proposal be laid before the heritors, who are intending to build a steeple here, that the Lodge will contribute to the building of a Lodge-room, as the basis of that steeple; and that, from the funds of the Lodge, they offer fifteen pounds, besides what will be advanced from the particular friends of the Lodge. In order that this proposal be properly laid before the heritors, five persons, namely the Right Worshipful Master, Brother McMath, Brother Burns, Brother Wodrow, Brother William Andrew – are appointed to meet on Saturday at one o'clock, to draw up a proposal to lay before the heritors on Friday first.

What became of the proposal is unknown. There is no record of the lodge ever having assembled in the base of the proposed steeple.

In all Burns signed twenty-nine minutes as Depute Master, and three are wholly his penmanship. He also subscribed his initials to a postscript. One of these signatures was stolen and never recovered. A second attempt was made to steal another part of the precious volume, but the theft was discovered in time and the stolen portion returned. It can be seen neatly pasted in its original setting. This minute book is, of course, of especial interest and is fully preserved in the lodge which also treasures the Master's chair, footstool, apron and the mallet used by him when presiding at its meetings, the candlesticks and other articles associated with him during his term of office. Also to be seen is an old Tyler's sword. The lodge Bible, which bears the date 1775, was one of the poet's possessions and was presented to the lodge by his brother Gilbert and himself. It was purchased by the lodge on 29 July 1786. The Minute reads – 'Bible cost 13s, lettering (*ie* the printed name of the lodge outside) cost 3s.' The Lodge has also the oft-quoted letter addressed by him from Edinburgh to his lodge brethren, prior to his Highland tour, intimating the reason for his inability to be present at one of their important meetings.

At this point it might be interesting and enlightening to enumerate some of the Rules applicable to St James's Lodge in Burns's day:

> At the third stroke of the Grand Master's hammer silence shall be maintained under a penalty of twopence.

Whosoever shall break a drinking glass at any meeting shall be liable to the instant payment of sixpence sterling for it, and the same sum for every other he may break before he leaves the room or company.

Those not at meetings within an hour of the fixed time shall be fined twopence.

If any Brother be so unfortunate as to have disordered his senses by strong liquors and thereby rendered himself incapable of behaving himself decently, peaceably and kind towards those around him, such Brother coming to the Lodge in that condition to the disturbance and disgust of his Brethren, shall be prudently ordered away to some place of safety in the meantime, and at the next meeting shall submit to such censure and admonition from the Chair, and to such a fine inflicted by the Lodge on him as to them may appear proper to his crime, and deter him from it in all time coming.

Whereas a Lodge always means a company of worthy men and circumspect, gathered together in order to promote charity, friendship, civility and good neighbourhood, it is enacted that no member of this Lodge shall speak slightingly, detractingly or calumniously of any of his Brethren behind their backs, so as to damage them in their professions without any certain grounds, and any member committing any such offence must humble himself by asking on his knees the pardon of such person or persons as his folly or malice hath aggrieved. Obstinate refusal to comply with this rule of the Brethren assembled shall be met with expulsion from the Lodge with every mark of ignominy and disgrace that is consistent with Justice and Freemasonry.

The excellent manner in which Burns carried out his duties may be gauged not only from his attendance record and his care of the Minutes of Proceedings, but also from the following letter written by Professor Dugaid Stewart.

In the summer of 1787 I passed some weeks in Ayrshire, and saw Burns occasionally . . . I was led by curiosity to attend for an hour or two a Masonic Lodge in Mauchline, where Burns presided. He had occasion to make some short unpremeditated compliments to different individuals from whom he had no occasion to expect a visit, and everything he said was happily conceived and forcibly as well as fluently expressed. His manner of speaking in public had evidently the marks of some practice in extempore elocution.

Professor Dugaid Stewart, who was then residing in Catrine, was admitted an honorary member of St James's Lodge, and the minute recording his admission was signed 'Robert Burns, D.M.' The Professor was a member of Lodge Canongate Kilwinning and proved himself a very good friend to the poet during his residence in Edinburgh and according to Burns was 'the most perfect character I ever saw.' Their early morning walks on the Braid Hills were greatly enjoyed by both.

During his term of office as Depute Master the Brethren were convened no fewer than seventy times, at thirty-three of which he was present, and his attendances would doubtless have been more numerous had he not been away from the district for lengthy periods in these two momentous years, 1787–1788.

It is generally believed that he visited a number of Lodges in his immediate vicinity. At a meeting on 27 March 1786, one lodge Loudin Kilwinning Newmilns, of which his friend Gavin Hamilton was Master, he was introduced to the Brethren and 'much to the satisfaction of the Lodge', was admitted a member, Brother John Morton being 'answrable for' his Admission money'.

A writer in the *Burns Chronicle* of 1893 states that the poet was present at a Mason Lodge held at Sorn on 5 October 1786, and in the same Annual for 1905 we have it that he 'mixed with the Brethren of the Craft in St Andrew's Lodge in Irvine', and that 'it is conjectured that it was in that town' that the 'stanra added in a Mason Lodge' was tacked on to his bacchanallian song, whose refrain is the 'big-bellied bottle'

> Then fill up a bumper, and make it o'erflow,
> And honours Masonic prepare for to throw,
> May every true Brother of the Compass and Square,
> Here a big-bellied bottle when harass'd with care!

Notwithstanding the long distance he had to travel he never found the road to and from the lodge wearisome. The thought of the meeting ahead and poetical composition so intruded into his mind that the miles would seem shorter. Masonic thoughts which are easily detectable in his poems can no doubt be traced to these evening walks. It has been said that Burns's attendances at masonic meetings led him into excesses. His brother Gilbert's testimony on this point is surely an effective answer to those who would cast this slur on the poet:

> Towards the end of the period under review (in his twenty-fourth year), and soon after his father's death, he was furnished with the subject of his epistle to John Rankin. During this period, also, he became a Freemason, which was his first introduction to the life of a boon companion. Yet, notwithstanding these circumstances, and the praise he has bestowed on Scotch Drink (which seems to have misled his historians) I do not recollect during these seven years, nor till towards the end of his commencing author (when his growing celebrity occasioned his often being in company), to have ever seen him intoxicated; nor was he at all given to drinking.

By this time Burns had become recognised as an outstanding poet, and his poems had been well received by those who heard them. It was during the winter of 1785–1786 that the full strength of his genius shone forth as at no other time. His poems were known to comparatively few, however, but among those few were the members of his own lodge, and they from the first recognised the poet's merits. On the suggestion of Gavin Hamilton, a lawyer, and landlord of Mossgiel Farm, Burns was persuaded to collect his writings and publish them by subscription, and so early in 1786 he went to Kilmarnock to arrange for this being done. He took up the suggestion with enthusiasm, and it is not too much to say that the brethren of his lodge were, out of friendship to their brother mason, largely responsible for the first edition of his poems. The brethren of St John's Lodge, Kilmarnock, which he frequently visited, also assisted very handsomely by subscribing freely themselves and getting others to supplement their action. They agreed to take 350 copies as soon as they were printed, the Right Worshipful Master subscribing for 35 copies and another brother for 75. This volume might with every justification be called a Masonic Edition. Burns himself could not find the means to publish it, but his masonic brethren loyally supported him in ensuring the success of the venture, which was, as might be expected, dedicated to Gavin Hamilton. John Wilson, an enthusiastic mason, was the printer of this First Edition. It cannot fail to be noticed that contact with freemasons and freemasonry runs like a golden thread throughout the poet's life, and the friends he met in the Craft had no small share in shaping his destiny. Well may Scottish Masons claim to have 'deserved well of humanity', for they saved from oblivion these gems of poetry and song which came from 'the soul of a man'.

Meantime he was having serious domestic troubles, Jean Armour and Mary Campbell had entered into his life, and his farming losses were heavy. The Highland Mary episode wherein Mary Campbell and Robert Burns enacted their betrothal, on opposite banks of the River Ayr, with ritualistic ceremony had a masonic touch about it: vows of fidelity were pronounced, Bibles exchanged, the names of the contracting parties being written on the fly-leaves, along with Burns's Masonic Mark with, on the one leaf, 'And ye shall not swear by my name falsely. . . . I am the Lord' from LEVITICUS, Chap. xix., v. 12, and on the other, 'Thous shalt not forswear thyself, but shalt perform unto the Lord thine oaths' from St MATTHEW, Chap. v., v. 33. This historic Bible with the signatures erased and part of the 'Mark' obliterated fell into the hands of a relative of Mary Campbell after her death, was purchased in Canada for £25, and may be seen in the Burns Museum in the monument on the banks of the Doon.

Burns was so weighed down by despondency that it was in the hope of bettering his position that he made up his mind on 12 June to proceed to Jamaica to take up an appointment there. One can easily understand in what stress he must have been when he entertained such a thought. Freemasonry had taught him 'ever to remember that the Almighty had implanted in his breast a sacred attachment towards that country whence he derived his birth and infant nurture'. In his early years he had again and again nourished the hope that he would 'for puir auld Scotland's sake' make 'some usefu' plan or book' or 'sing a sang at least'.

He was re-elected to the Depute Mastership on 16 June 1786, his brother Gilbert going into the Senior Warden's Chair. It is rather curious that he should have allowed his name to go forward on that date for re-election to this office as he had already set his mind on Jamaica, and on 23 June he recited his 'Farewell to the Brethren of St James's Lodge.' This meeting was probably that to which he had sent his poetical invitation to his doctor, Dr Mackenzie of Mauchline.

> Friday first's the day appointed
> By our Right Worshipful anointed,
>   To hold our grand procession;
> To get a blad o' Johnny's morals,
> And taste a swatch o' Manson's barrels
>   I' the way of our profession.
>
> Our Master and the Brotherhood
>   Would a' be glad to see you;
> For me I would be mair than proud
>   To share the mercies wi' you.
>   If Death, then, wi' skaith, then,
>   Some mortal heart is hechtin',
>   Inform him, and storm him,
>   That Saturday you'll fecht him.

The 'Day appointed' was the anniversary of St John the Baptist, and this was observed by the brethren walking in procession. It was 'Carnival day in Tarbolton'. As Midsummer Day was one of the few occasions on which freemasonry came before the public, Burns was especially anxious that there should be a good muster of the brethren and so used to address the members personally. The poem quoted above has been preserved with the signature 'Robert Burns, D.M.' and dated from 'Mossgiel, 14 June, AM 1790'.

The famous Kilmarnock Edition of his poems was published on 31 July, met with instant success, and he suddenly leapt into fame. The whole 600 copies were bought up in the matter of a few weeks, he himself being richer by £20. What these volumes are worth today it would be difficult to assess.

His passage to Jamaica had been booked. His vessel was due to sail at the end of November. He had written his 'Farewell to the Brethren', and Scotland seemed on the point of losing her illustrious son, when a letter written by Doctor Blacklock to a friend, and which Burns received, caused him to change his mind, overthrow all his schemes, and remain in his native land, where new prospects to his poetic ambition were opened up. To quote his own words:

> I had just taken the last farewell of a few friends; my chest was on the road to Greenock; I had composed the last song I should ever measure in Caledonia; when Dr Blacklock's opinion that I would meet with encouragement in Edinburgh for a second edition fired me so much that I posted away to that city.

This 'last song' was 'The gloomy night is gathering fast'. Had Burns's intention to emigrate been fulfilled it is more than likely that his great 'Farewell' poem would have concluded his active connection with Scottish Freemasonry.

> Adieu! a heart-warm, fond adieu
>   Dear brothers of the mystic tie!
> Ye favour'd, ye enlighten'd few,
>   Companions of my social joy!
> Tho' I to foreign lands must hie,
>   Pursuing Fortune's slidd'ry ba',
> With melting heart, and brimful eye,
>   I'll mind you still, tho' far awa'.
>
> Oft have I met your social band,
>   And spent the cheerful festive night;
> Oft honour'd with supreme command,
>   Presided o'er the sons of light;
> And by that hieroglyphic bright,
>   Which none but craftsmen ever saw!
> Strong mem'ry on my heart shall write
>   Those happy scenes when far awa'.
>
> May freedom, harmony and love,
>   Unite you in the grand design,
> Beneath th'omniscient eye above,
>   The glorious architect divine!
> That you may keep th'unerring line,
>   Still rising by the plummet's law,
> Till order bright completely shine,
>   Shall be my prayer when far awa'.

> And you, farewell! whose merits claim,
> Justly that highest badge to wear!
> Heav'n bless your honour'd, noble name,
> To masonry and Scotia dear!
> A last request, permit me here,
> When yearly ye assemble a',
> One round, I ask it with a tear,
> To him, the bard that's far awa'!

Some of his biographers have stated that by the time he reached the last stanza many of the brethren were in tears.

The person entitled to wear the 'Highest Badge' was the Master of the Lodge, and the Master of St James's at that date was Captain, afterwards Major-General James Montgomerie, a younger brother of Colonel Hugh Montgomerie, afterwards Earl of Eglinton. Some authorities assert that the reference is to the Grand Master Mason of Scotland, William Wallace, Sheriff of Ayr. The poet's request to be remembered yearly at the festive board is regularly honoured in St James's Lodge.

On 26 October Burns was made an honourary member of Kilmarnock Kilwinning St John, No 24 (now No 22), which met in the old Commercial Inn, now demolished, in Croft Street. He was pleased at the honour conferred upon him and in recognition wrote the stanzas beginning 'Ye sons of Old Killie, assembled by Willie,' the Christian name of the reigning Master whose name appears at the close of the following Minute:

> Oct 26th, 1786.
> Present the Right Worshipful Master, Deputy Master and several Brethren, when John Galt, farmer, in Cressland, was, upon his petition, made and entered Apprentice. At same time Robert Burns, poet, Mauchline, a member of St James's, Tarbolton, was made an honorary member of this Lodge.
> (Signed)   WILL PARKER

> Ye sons of Old Killie, assembled by Willie,
> To follow the noble vocation
> Your thrifty old mother has scarce such another
> To sit in that honoured station.

> Within this dear Mansion, may wayward Contention
> Or withered Envy ne'er enter;
> May Secrecy round be the mystical bound,
> And brotherly Love be the Centre!

Several lodges now began to recognise the genius of the poet and also to show their appreciation of the man. In this connection it is noteworthy that Kilmarnock Kilwinning conferred on him his first honorary membership, and it was the first occasion on which he is described as a poet. This lodge has amongst its many treasured possessions a Master's mallet presented to the lodge by Burns, and a holograph letter from Sir Walter Scott. Here is a copy of the letter:

> Sir, – I am much gratified by the sight of the portrait of Robert Burns. I saw that distinguished poet only once, and that many years since, and being a bad marker of likenesses and recollector of faces, I should in an ordinary case have hesitated to offer an opinion upon the resemblance, especially as I make no pretension to judge of the fine arts. But Burns was so remarkable a man that his features remain impressed on my mind as I had seen him only yesterday, and I could not hesitate to recognise this portrait as a striking resemblance of the poet, though it had been presented to me amid a whole exhibition.
> I am, sir,
> Your obedient servant,
> WALTER SCOTT
>
> Edinburgh, 14 November (1829).

Burns presided at a meeting of his lodge on 10 November 1786, soon after which he set his face towards Edinburgh, reaching there on 28 November and taking up his residence with his friend John Richmond in Baxter's Close, Lawnmarket. In the metropolis he was to spend some of the happiest moments of his life, and these were closely bound up with freemasonry. Two days after his arrival the Grand Lodge of Scotland celebrated the Festival of Saint Andrew. The brethren assembled in the aisle of St Giles and walked in procession to St Andrew's Church, where a masonic service was conducted. Burns may have been in that procession as invitations were issued to brethren of country lodges requesting their presence at the function. Shortly after his arrival in the city he was introduced to Lodge Canongate Kilwinning by Brother James Dalrymple of Orangefield near Ayr, and who had previously known the poet. He is reputed to have attended a meeting of this lodge on 7 December, but Brother D. Murray Lyon does not admit to definite evidence on the point. If he was there, and whether or not, he met Lord Glencairn and the Hon Henry Erskine, both introduced by Brother Dalrymple. Of these three brethren Burns writes in terms of the highest praise. In conversation with his friend Gavin Hamilton the same evening, he says:

> I am in a fair way to becoming as eminent as Thomas à Kempis or John Bunyan. . . . My Lord Glencairn and the Dean of Faculty, Mr H. Erskine, have taken me under their wing; and by all probability I shall soon be the tenth worthy, and the eighth wise man of the world. . . . I have met in Mr Dalrymple, of Orangefield, what Solomon emphatically calls 'A friend that sticketh closer than a brother'.

The Earl of Glencairn never lost interest in Burns. He introduced him to Creech the publisher, secured the patronage of the Caledonian Hunt, did everything in his power to obtain subscribers among the nobility, and used his influence to get Burns into the Excise. Burns was not the man to allow this kindness to pass without showing his appreciation. Some three years later Glencairn died, and when the poet learned of this he wrote to the factor in these words:

> Dare I trouble you to let me know privately before the day of interment, that I may cross the country and steal among the crowd to pay a tear to the last sight of my ever revered benefactor?

And in addition to this he composed in his 'Lament for James, Earl of Glencairn' one of the finest stanzas he ever wrote:

> The bridegroom may forget the bride
>   Was made his wedded wife yestreen;
> The monarch may forget the crown
>   That on his head an hour has been;
> The mother may forget the bairn
>   That smiles sae sweetly on her knee;

But I'll remember thee, Glencairn,
And a' that thou hast done for me!

In Edinburgh he was to find many of the literati who thought highly of him. Principal Robertson, for example, owned that he scarcely ever met any man whose conversation displayed more intellectual vigour. Dugald Stewart's reference to him has already been noted. Dalzel, Professor of Greek in Edinburgh University says:

> We have a poet in town just now, whom everybody is taking notice of – a ploughman from Ayrshire – a man of unquestionable genius. He runs the risk of being spoiled by the excessive attention paid him just now by persons of all ranks. Those who know him best say he has too much good sense to allow himself to be spoiled.

Burns's fame was now rapidly growing and he threw himself zealously into the work of publishing a second and enlarged volume of his poems. He was to find that the masonic associations which had proved so helpful in the issue of his Kilmarnock Edition were to stand him in good stead again. These friends were practically all members of Lodge Canongate Kilwinning.

He definitely visited Lodge St Andrew on 12 January 1787, on the occasion of a visitation from Grand Lodge when the Grand Master Charteris unexpectedly gave the toast 'Caledonia and Caledonia's Bard, Brother Burns.' The following day Brother John Ballantine of Ayr received this letter from the poet describing his visit to the Lodge:

> I went to a Mason Lodge yesternight where the Most Worshipful Grand Master Charteris and all the Grand Lodge of Scotland visited. The meeting was most numerous and elegant; all the different Lodges about town were present in all their pomp. The Grand Master, who presided with great solemnity, and honour to himself as a Gentleman and Mason, among other general toasts gave 'Caledonia and Caledonia's Bard, Brother Burns,' which rung through the whole Assembly with multiplied honours and repeated acclamations. As I had no idea such a thing would happen, I was downright thunderstruck, and trembling in every nerve made the best return in my power. Just as I finished, some of the Grand

Officers said so loud as I could hear, with a most comforting accent, 'Very well indeed,' which set me something to rights again.

Two weeks afterwards, on 1 February, we find him in Canongate Kilwinning Lodge, surrounded by some of the literary personalities of Edinburgh, and there he was affiliated as set forth in the following short Minute:

> The Right Worshipful Master (Alexander Fergusson of Craigdarroch) having observed that Brother Burns was at present in the Lodge, who is well known as a great poetic writer, and for a late publication of his works, which have been universally commended, and submitted that he should be assumed a member of this Lodge, which was unanimously agreed to, and he was assumed accordingly.

The Minute concludes thus:

> Having spent the evening in a very social manner, as the meetings of the Lodge always have been, it was adjourned till next monthly meeting,

It was at this meeting on 1 March that Burns is supposed to have been installed as Poet Laureate. The Minute of 1 February went upon the Lodge-Book, and it is preserved today in the lodge among its choicest treasures. The meeting on 1 February was, so far as is known, the last masonic meeting attended by Burns in Edinburgh, if we omit the ceremony of the Poet Laureateship on 1 March, about which there has been so much dispute. The matter has never been satisfactorily cleared up. Lodge books in those days were very imperfectly kept. Many of the Minutes were not even signed. For example, there is no Minute in the St Andrew's Lodge Books that Burns was ever in that lodge, and his visit there might never have been remembered had he not happened to refer to it in the letter already quoted to one of his friends.

With regard to the much discussed meeting of Lodge Canongate Kilwinning on 1 March 1787, it has been assumed that the business which was to have come before the meeting was in the first place to send a letter of congratulation to the Prince of Wales, who had on 6 February been initiated into the mysteries of freemasonry at the Star and Garter, London, and secondly to confer a mark of respect on Robert Burns. But the Minute in question as it appears in the Canongate Kilwinning records reads:

> St John's Chapel, 1st March 1787. – The Lodge being duly constituted, it was reported that since last meeting (and here follow the names of newly made Entered Apprentices and Fellows of Craft) 'no other business being before the meeting the Lodge adjourned.'

No word here of Burns's installation as Poet Laureate nor of any congratulatory epistle to the Prince of Wales.

Was he referring to the Laureateship when he penned the following lines in acknowledgement of a present from a friend?

> But Latin Willie's reek noo raise (Willie Nicol)
> He'd seen that nicht *Rab crown'd wi' bays.*

It would appear that as far as Lodge Canongate is concerned the first reference to Burns's inauguration to the Poet Laureateship was not until 1815, when the Brethren were asked to subscribe to the fund for the erection of the Mausoleum of Burns who, they said, 'had been Poet Laureate to the Lodge', this being followed in 1835 when James Hogg, the Ettrick Shepherd, was elected to succeed Burns as Poet Laureate, acknowledged the honour conferred upon him as well as the compliment of being Burns's successor. The brethren drank to the memory of Burns as 'the last Poet Laureate of the Lodge'. If any of those who were members of the lodge in 1787 were present on either or both of these dates they must have known the facts. Certain it is that the statements were never contradicted.

An interesting correspondence between Brother H. C. Peacock, Secretary of the Lodge, and Brother D. Murray Lyon is to be found in *The History of the Lodge Canongate Kilwinning, No 2*, by Allan Mackenzie, RWM, in 1883–1887, regarding the controversy.

The Edinburgh Edition of Burns's poems was published on 21 April 1787, from the publishing shop of Mr Creech, in the

Luckenbooths. It was in a handsome octavo volume, price five shillings. Creech's advertisement contained the following note:

> As the book is published for the sole benefit of the author, it is requested that subscribers will send for their copies: and none will be delivered without money.

The Kilmarnock Preface was abandoned and in its place appeared a

DEDICATION
TO THE NOBLEMEN AND GENTLEMEN
OF THE CALEDONIAN HUNT

and then follows the Preface by Burns. The list of Subscribers extended to over thirty-eight pages comprising 1,500 persons subscribing for 2,800 copies. Many of them were members of Canongate Kilwinning. Smellie, his printer, Creech, his publisher, and Naysmith, who provided the frontispiece to his works, were all masons. In that connection it has been said that 'surely never book came out of a more Masonic laboratory'. It was, too, his brother mason, John Ballantyne of Ayr who, hearing that poverty prevented the publication of a second edition of his poems offered to lend him the money required for the purpose.

> Affliction's sons are brothers in distress;
> A brother to relieve, how exquisite the bliss.

There is no doubt that his connection with freemasonry in Edinburgh was the most interesting and to him the most enjoyable period of his life, and it was during the few months spent there that his genius was appreciated and rewarded.

After having spent about five months in the capital he set out on 6 May 1787 on a tour to the South of Scotland with Mr Robert Ainslie, a young lawyer, to whom he had been introduced at a masonic meeting. They visited a number of interesting spots and met several distinguished people. On 7 May they reached Coldstream and crossed the border into England. Burns's love for his native land overcame him here and he could not refrain from uttering aloud, with deep emotion and devotion, the two concluding stanzas of 'The Cottar's Saturday Night', four of the lines being:

> O Scotia! my dear, my native soil!
>   For whom my warmest wish to Heaven is sent!
> Long may thy hardy sons of rustic toil
>   Be blest with health and peace and sweet content!

On 18 May they arrived at Eyemouth where, through the influence of their host, a meeting of the lodge was convened for the next day, and there Burns and Ainslie were made Royal Arch Masons, as set forth in the following Minute:

> 'Eyemouth, 19th May 1787.
> At a general encampment held ... in Lodge St Ebbe, the following Brethren were made Royal Arch Masons – namely Robert Burns ... and Robert Ainslie. ... Robert Ainslie paid one guinea admission dues: but on account of R. Burns's remarkable poetical genius, the encampment unanimously agreed to admit him gratis, and considered themselves honoured by having a man of such shining abilities for one of their companions.

The members of the lodge forming this 'general encampment' secured an English Charter some three months later authorising them to be erected into a Chapter, bearing the name of 'Land of Cakes' R.A. Chapter, No 52, on the English Roll. The Chapter is now Scottish, No 15.

Having parted with Ainslie he crossed the north of England to Dumfries, where he stayed two days and was presented with the freedom of the burgh. Ayr and Mossgiel were reached on 9 June and ten days later he was re-elected Deputy Master of his lodge, but there is no record of his being at the meeting and the Minute is unsigned. St James's Lodge sometimes met by deputation at Mauchline. On 25 July he presided at a meeting there, honorary membership being conferred on several well-known Masons, including Professor Dugald Stewart, who had on more than one occasion befriended the poet.

In the early days of August Burns returned to Edinburgh to settle with his publisher. An important meeting of his lodge was due, and he found himself unable to be present. He accordingly sent the following letter to his Tarbolton Lodge, addressed 'Men and Brethren' and with the date 'Edinburgh, 23 August 1787:

> I am truly sorry it is not in my power to be at your quarterly meeting. If I must be absent in body, believe me I shall be present in spirit. I suppose those who owe us monies, by bill or otherwise, will appear – I mean those we summoned. If you please, I wish you would delay prosecuting defaulters till I come home. The court is up, and I will be home before it sits down. In the meantime to take a note of who appear and who do not, of our faulty debtors, will be right in my humble opinion; and those who confess debt and crave days, I think we should spare them. Farewell!
>
>   Within your dear Mansion may wayward Contention
>   Or withered Envy ne'er enter;
>   May Secrecy round be the mystical bound,
>   And brotherly Love be the Center!!!
>
>   ROBERT BURNS.

The quatrain above it will be recalled was the last of the verses he wrote to Lodge Kilmarnock Kilwinning on his receiving honorary membership there. One word only was changed, viz.: 'your' replacing 'their' in the first line.

Two days later he set out on his Highland tour with Willie Nicol, immortalised as having 'brewed a peck o' maut,' said to be the greatest drinking song in any language. They reached beyond Inverness, travelling in all nearly 600 miles over a period of twenty-two days, and meeting many masonic brethren en route. Tradition has it that he was made an honorary member of Lodge Ancient Brazen, No 17, Linlithgow, but there is no record of this having taken place. Lodge Stirling Ancient, No 30, also believes that he attended a meeting of the brethren and entered his name in the Attendance Book. This register used to be displayed to visitors, but on one occasion it was found that the page containing the poet's signature had been removed, and at a subsequent date the register too disappeared. This would almost indicate that he was in reality a visitor there. Their arrival in Edinburgh on 16 September completed the tour.

Burns spent the winter in the capital prodding his publisher for a settlement. When this was squared he found himself enriched to the extent of £500. He was also in communication with Brother Patrick Millar of Dalswinton for a lease of the farm of Ellisland, and at the same time was seeking, through the good offices of one of his brother masons, an appointment in the Excise. There is very little documentary evidence to show that he interested himself in masonry during this second Edinburgh period, though it has been asserted that he attended many meetings during these five months. On one occasion he states in an undated letter that 'to-night the Grand Master and lodge of Masons appear at the Theatre in form. I am determined to go to the play. . . . I will call on you a few minutes before the Theatre opens.' Members of the Craft were patrons of the Drama and when a particular play was on they were wont to appear in full masonic regalia.

Burns returned to Mossgiel in March 1788, married Jean Armour in April, and lent his brother Gilbert £200 to ease the condition of his widowed mother and her family. He attended his Lodge on 7 and 23 May, the latter occasion being the last time he signed the Minute as Depute Master. It is reputed that he foregathered with the brethren on 24 June, on the occasion of the annual masonic procession. A few days before, on 13 June, he had taken possession of Ellisland, but does not seem to have been enamoured with the idea of residing in Dumfriesshire, for in a letter to his friend Hugh Parker, lamenting the fact that he was missing his Ayrshire friends he pens a verse concluding with:

> Tarbolton, twenty-fourth of June
> Ye'll find me in a better tune.

Another fact of regret to him was that there was not a 'kenn'd face' in the district except his auld mare, Jenny Geddes:

> Dowie she saunters doon Nithside
> And aye a westlin' leuk she throws
> While tears hap ower her auld broon nose.

On this 24 of June James Findlay, a fellow exciseman, was appointed Depute Master in succession to the poet, the Master being James Dalrymple of Orangefield, who has already been referred to as befriending Burns while in Edinburgh.

He paid flying visits to Mauchline on 21 October and 11 November, when his lodge met under his presidency. This was the last meeting of St James's Lodge he attended and his association with this lodge which he so much adorned was at an end.

While at Ellisland his masonic interest was renewed. He affiliated to Lodge St Andrew, Dumfries, No 179, erected in 1774, and with this lodge he retained his connection to the end. It became known as 'Burns's Lodge'. His affiliation fee was 10s. The Minute which records his admission is a quaint one and full of inaccuracies, both as to spelling and figures:

> The Brethren having selebrated the Anniversary of St John in the usual manner and Brother Burns in Aellisland of St Davids Strabolton Lodge, No. 178, being present The Lodge unanimously assumed him a member of the Lodge being a Master Masson he subscribed the regulations as a member Thereafter the Lodge was shut.
>
> Signed SIM MACKENZIE.

The next mention of the poet is made in the Minute of 28 December 1789, when his name appears on the list of those present, and as having made payment, along with the other members, of his quarterly fees. Then again he is one of five brethren who met in the Globe Tavern, Dumfries, in April 1790, when as usual friendships were established, one of his friends presenting him with an apron of

> chamois leather, very fine, with figures of gold, some of them relieved with green, others with a dark red colour (while) on the under side of the semi-circular part which is turned down at the top is written in bold, fair hand: Charles Sharpe, of Hotham, to Rabbie Burns, Dumfries, Dec. 12, 1791.

Burns and Sharpe were mutually interested in music and verse.

His next appearance was at the meeting on 19 April 1791, but for some reason the blank space left for the Minute was never filled in. On 27 December of the same year, and on 6 February and 14 May 1792, he was again present at meetings of the lodge when he acted as Steward. On 31 May of that year he took part in the proceedings, part of which was ordering the clerk to procure 'a proper silver seal for the use of the Lodge'. On 5 June he appears again. As he was now resident in Dumfries, having given up the farm at Ellisland, it was more convenient and easier for him to be present at lodge meetings. He attended again on 22 and 30 November of that year, and at the latter meeting (St Andrew's Day), was elected to the Senior Warden's chair, which office he filled for a year. Exactly a year later 'The Senior Warden' (Burns) is noted as being present. His name does not appear again until 29 November 1794, when the election of office-bearers took place, and over a year elapses ere his name is mentioned on the sederunt, when on 28 January 1796 he stood sponsor for a candidate 'a merchant in Liverpool who, being recommended by Burns, was admitted apprentice'. At this meeting the Brethren agreed that the new Apprentice's 'fees be applied towards defraying the expenses of this night'. While a member of St Andrew's Lodge, out of a possible 16 meetings he was present at 11 of them. His final attendance was on 14 April 1796.

The state of Burn's health at this time was such that Robert Chambers in his *Life of Burns*, speaking of these last two meetings says, 'It is not unlikely that both on this occasion (14 April) and on the 28 of January Burns made an effort, if not a sacrifice, for the honour of persons whom he regarded as friends'. The lodge records contain no reference to his death, though we may be sure the members paid tribute and respect to the memory of one who had assisted so often in their masonic labours.

The lodge ceased to meet in 1805, and an attempt was made in 1815 to revive it, when the Minute closes with a resolution to support the Provincial Grand Master now William Millar of Dalswinton, at laying the foundation stone (on 5 June) of the Mausoleum to be erected over the remains of Robert Burns, the most distinguished Brother that St Andrew's Lodge had been privileged to receive within its portals. Several lodges attended the ceremony, but St Andrew is not mentioned as being represented, although over 400 freemasons took part in the proceedings. Efforts to revive it proved futile and no other meetings are recorded. It was struck off the roll of the Grand Lodge of Scotland in 1816. No reference is made in any of the other lodges, meeting regularly while Burns lived in Dumfries, to his having paid them any visits, though no doubt he took his share in their proceedings from time to time, and thus it is to the precious Minute Book of the lodge alone that we are indebted for some knowledge of the masonic activities of our national poet during his stay in Dumfries.

In December 1879, at a public sale, certain articles, once the property of lodge St Andrew, No 179, were purchased and paid for by the then Grand Master Mason, Sir Michael Shaw Stewart, Baronet, who presented them to the Grand Lodge of Scotland. There were – (1) The Minute Book of Lodge St Andrew, Dumfries, No 179, of which Burns was an affiliated member, bearing the poet's signature to the Bye-laws and containing the Minute of his admission; (2) the mallet of St Andrew's, and an apron used in the lodge in Burns's time. These are on exhibit in the Grand Lodge Museum.

In this brief survey of the masonic activities of our national poet some minor details have been omitted, but perhaps sufficient has been written to show that in the short span of life vouchsafed to him Robert Burns proved himself an adornment to the Fraternity of which he was one of the most illustrious members.

5

THE CABLE-TOW

W. Graham Brown

AMONG THE MANY symbols and veiled verbal references which occur in ceremonies of Entering, Passing and Raising there are some which are less easy of interpretation than others. Of some it may be said that it can be interpreted by a child, but such an interpretation is likely to be incorrect and it is probably true to say the real symbolism lies much deeper than would at first sight appear. The Cable-tow is one of these symbols. In the Entered Apprentice Degree the aspirant is taught the useful lesson that he who has once felt within him the impulses of Light, and been moved to seek it, should never retreat from his quest, and, indeed, cannot do so without doing violence to the highest within him, a violence equivalent to moral suicide.

At the same time he is also enjoined not to be unduly precipitate, not ignorantly and rashly rush forward in an unprepared inward state to grasp the secrets of his own being, in which case peril of another kind threatens him; but to proceed humbly, meekly, cautiously and under instructed guidance. The ancient maxim 'Know thyself', was coupled with another, *Ne quid nimis*, 'Nothing in Excess'; for the science can only be learned and applied gradually. It will unfold itself more and more as it is diligently studied and pursued.

The foregoing explanation of the cable-tow is but a very partial one, and inculcates a salutary, but purely moral, piece of advice. The deeper significance is a psycho-physiological one, and has to do with the mysteries of the human organism. It should not be overlooked that the cable-tow is given prominence not only in the first degree. It is again mentioned in the obligation in the third degree, whilst it appears under another guise in the working-tool of the Master Mason which acts upon a centre pin. And finally it reappears in the Royal Arch Degree as a cord or life line. It is requisite to understand what is involved in something to which such recurring prominence is given.

Let us first recall what has been already stated about the human organism being a composite structure of several natures or bodies (physical, etheric, emotional, and mental), fixated in a unity or synthesis; each of such bodies being constituted of gross or subtle matter, of differing density and vibratory rate, and the whole co-ordinated by the central divine principle (which may or may not yet have come forward into the formal conscious mind, although there are few in whose awareness it is not lurkingly present and more or less active as 'conscience').

Thus the human constitution may be likened to a number of glass tumblers placed one within the other and with, say, a night light (representing the central Principle) inserted in the inmost one. The glass of the tumblers may be imagined as of progressive thickness and coarseness, from within outwards, and some of them as coloured, dirty, or not closely fitting in with the others. The coarser, dirtier, and more opaque the glasses, the less able will be the central Light to shine through them; a single glass may be so opaque as to prevent the passage of the light through all the rest. Here, then, is an object lesson, in the need for the inward purification of our various constituent sheaths, and for becoming 'perfect in all our parts'. As William Blake said very truly: 'If the gates of human perception were thoroughly cleansed, we should perceive everything as it is – infinite; but man has closed himself up till he sees all things only through the narrow chinks of his own cavern.'

Another illustration. Human compositeness may be compared with the concentric skins or sheaths of a vegetable bulb (an onion, or hyacinth). Here the sheaths are all equally pure and co-ordinated; and because the bulb is perfect in all its parts of sheaths, and, when planted, fulfils the whole law of its nature, its life-force bursts its natural bonds, throws up a self-built superstructure into the air, and there effloresces into the bloom which is its 'crown of life' or fulness of development. Man should do this, and, as we have shown, this is what the Mason is taught to do. But man having (what the bulb has not), freedom of will to fulfil or to violate the law of his nature, has chosen the latter course, and consequently by indulgence in perverse desire and wrongly directed thought, has fouled and disorganised his sheaths. Hence his spiritual darkness and his liability to all forms of disease. The central Principle cannot shine through this opacity, lighting up his mind and governing his desires and actions. It remains imprisoned within him. He sees, thinks and knows only from his self-darkened outer sheaths, and is misguided and deluded accordingly.

For a final example, let us return to the instructive familiar episode in the Gospels of the storm overtaking a boat containing a number of men, of whom the Chief was 'asleep in the hinder part of the boat'. The boat typifies the human organism; its occupants, its various parts and faculties, including the as yet unawakened Master Principle resident in its depths or 'hinder part'. An emotional upheaval occurs; the rough waves of passion threaten to wreck the whole party. A brain storm arises; intemperate gusts of fright, wrong-headedness, and mental un-control, make the position still worse. The extremity is sufficiently acute to awaken the Master Principle into activity whose beneficent power is able instantly to still those unruly winds and waves, which suddenly are reduced to a great peace.

Every Master Mason, who is a real and not merely a titular one, is able to perform this 'miracle' in himself; perhaps in others also. There is nothing supernatural about it to him. It is possible to him because he 'has the Mason Word and second sight'; he both understands the composite structure of the human organism, can visually discern the disordered part or parts and can apply healing, harmonising, vibratory power from his own corresponding part to the seat of the mischief, saying to this disordered mental part or that unruly emotional sheath, 'Peace, be still'. Every Master Mason is therefore also a Master Physician, able to benefit patients in a medical sense, and also to visualise the inner condition of those who look to him for instruction and initiation in a Masonic sense, to advise upon their interior needs and moral ailments, and help them to purify and align their disordered natures. But this is not possible save to one who himself has become pure and rectified in all his parts; the physician must first heal himself before he can communicate either physical or moral health to others.

This promise about the compositeness of the human structure and the existence in us of a series of independent, yet co-ordinated 'parts' or sheaths, has been necessary before we can speak directly of the cable-tow. What is it that connects these parts? And are these parts dissociable from one another?

We know that they are normally in close association and to this association applies the enjoinder that what God hath joined, man shall not put asunder. What the age-long process of evolution has built up with infinite patience and care is not to be tampered with for improper purposes, or even by well-meaning but, as yet, unenlightened experiment in the supposed interests of science; a point upon which the old masters and teachers of our science are specially insistent, for reasons which now need not to be entered upon.

Nevertheless, a measure of dissociation does occur naturally in even the most healthy and well-organised people (and of cases of abnormal psychic looseness of constitution we need not speak). It occurs in sleep, when the consciousness may be vividly active, whether in an orderly or disorderly manner; people 'travel' in their sleep. It occurs at times of illness or violent shock. It may be induced by alcohol or drugs; the 'anaesthetic revelation' is a well recognised phenomenon. Under any of these conditions there may be a complete ekstasis, or conscious standing out or away of the ego from the physical body. Apparitions and even action at a distance are well accredited facts. Such phenomena are explicable only upon the suppositions of the existence of a subtler vehicle than the gross body, of the fact that consciousness becomes temporarily transferred from the latter to the former, and that the two are capable of conjoint function in complete independence of the physical brain and body.

What preserves the connection between the two parts thus disjoined, and makes possible their subsequent recoalescence, is the 'cable-tow'. It is a connecting thread of matter of extreme tenuousness and elasticity issuing from the physical abdominal region and maintaining the same kind of connection with the extended subtle body as the string with which a boy flies a kite. As the boy can pull in the kite by the string, so does the extruded subtle body become drawn back to its physical base. Were the kite string severed during the kite's flight, the kite would collapse or be blown away. Similarly, were the human 'cable-tow' permanently severed, death would ensue and each of the severed parts go to its own place.

Biblically this human 'cable-tow' is called the silver cord in the well-known passage, 'or ever the silver cord is loosed and the golden bowl is broken; then shall the body return to the earth and the spirit to God who gave it'. 'Silver' is the technical esoteric term for psychical substance, as gold is for spiritual, and iron or brass for physical. Its physiological correspondence is the umbilical cord connecting the child with its mother. Its analogue in ecclesiastical vestments is the girdle worn by the high priests of the Hebrew and by the priests and monastics of the Christian Church.

Everyone unconsciously possesses the cable-tow, and it comes into use during sleep, when a less or greater measure of involuntary dissociation of our parts occurs. A Master, however, is one who has outgrown the incapacities to which the undeveloped average man is subject. Unlike the latter, he is in full knowledge and control of all his parts; whether his physical body be awake or wrapped in sleep, he maintains unbroken consciousness. He is able at will to shut off consciousness of temporal affairs and apply it to supra-physical ones. He can thus function at a distance from his physical body, whether upon the mundane or upon higher planes of the cosmic ladder. His cable-tow, of infinite expansiveness, unwinds from his centre pin and, stretching like the kite string, enables him to travel where he will in his subtle body and to rejoin and reanimate his physical one at will. Hence it is that the Master Mason is pledged to answer and obey all signs and summonses from any Master Mason's lodge if within the reach of his cable-tow; and such assemblies, it should be remembered, are contemplated therefore as taking place not at any physical location, but upon an ethereal plane. For corroboration of what is possible in this respect to a Master, one should reflect upon the instances of bilocation, passing through closed walls, and manifesting at a distance, recorded of the Great Exemplar in the Gospels. These are representative of what is feasible to anyone attaining Mastership.

The cable-tow, therefore, is given prominence to the reflective Craftsman as a help towards understanding his own constitution, and to foreshadow to him work that lies before him when he is fitted to undertake it – work which now may seem to him impossible and incredible. For as the skirret (which is the cable-tow in another form) is intended for the skilful architect to draw forth a line to mark out the ground for the intended structure, so the competent builder of the spiritual body will unwind his own 'silver cord' when he learns how to function consciously on the ascending ladder of supra-physical planes, and to perceive the nature of the superstructure he himself is intended to construct.

Further importance attaches to the significance of the cable-tow from the fact testified to at the admission to our Order of every new candidate for ceremonial initiation. For all real Initiation involves the use of the actual 'silver cord' or life-line; since such Initiation always occurs when the physical body is in a state of trance or sleep, and when the temporarily liberated consciousness has been transferred to a higher level. Thence it subsequently is brought back to the physical organism, the cerebral and nerve centres of which become illumined, revitalised and raised to a higher pitch of faculty than was previously possible. The perspicacious Royal Arch Mason will not fail to perceive how this truth is dramatically exemplified in that degree.

This subject might be considerably extended, for whilst in a ceremonial system like freemasonry, only one initiation is portrayed (or rather where initiation only occurs once), yet in the actual experience of soul-architecture Initiation succeeds Initiation upon increasingly higher levels of the ladder as the individual becomes correspondingly ripe for them, able to bear their strain and to assimilate their revelations. What the Craft teaching and symbols inculcate is a principle common to every degree of real Initiation that one may prove worthy to attain. For each upward step, the candidate for the heights must be prepared as he is in the Entered Apprentice degree; at each there will be the same peril in turning back, and at each the same menace directed against rashly rushing forward.

6
BASIC PRINCIPLES OF MASONIC SYMBOLISM

Charles G. Reigner

FREEMASONRY DEALS WITH the fundamental issues of life. It is intended to make masons deeply aware of three basic truths – the Fatherhood of God, the Brotherhood of Man, and the Immortality of the Soul. Those phrases have been so much banded about and have become so commonplace with us that often we use them with but little thought of their deeper meaning. They embody truths on which thoughtful men have pondered through the ages. In a very real sense every person has to discover truth for himself. No thoughtful man is ever willing to be satisfied with what comes to him secondhand. 'What is Truth?' is always the question uppermost in the minds of thinking people.

Man differs from the creatures of the brute world because he has the God-given power to think. Far too often he fails to use that power in the deeper concerns of his life. He becomes so occupied with the things that he can see and feel and hear and touch that the higher values of life have little or no meaning for him. The disturbed conditions of our time grow out of the fact that far too many people are wholly concerned with the physcial aspects of life. 'How can I get?' not 'How can I give?' is the ruling passion of great masses of men.

Next to the Church and the home, freemasonry has been for some of us the most beneficent influence in our lives. That influence grows out of an ever-deepening understanding of the symbolic teaching of freemasonry – an understanding that cannot be developed when a Mason is wholly occupied with the externals of the lodge – its offices, its jewels, its business, even the verbatim repetition of the ritual.

Work in freemasonry is a labour of love. The labour involved in writing Masonic books and articles – even this paper – is done without the hope of fee or material reward. The basic purpose of Masonic writing is to share with other Masons the outcome of Masonic study and contemplation. Without a firm conviction on the part of Masonic students and writers of the worthwhileness of Masonic study, there would be not literature of freemasonry.

In the study of freemasonry there are three main divisions – its history, its symbolism, and its governing laws. The symbolism of freemasonry is its soul. Right in that sentence we have an illustration of what we mean by symbolism. Sometimes we say that a man whom we admire is 'the very soul of honour'. By that statement we mean that his whole life is controlled and activated by a sense of virtue – of honour.

We may refer to someone as being a thoroughly 'heartless' man. Obviously we do not mean that his body does not contain the physical organ which we call the heart; rather, we mean to imply that he is 'heartless' because he is cruel and selfish in his attitude and actions. Time and time again we use the word heart to refer to our emotional nature, just as we use the word soul to mean our spiritual nature.

Again, we may say that in a certain factory or plant so many 'hands' are employed. Everybody understands that by that expression we mean the number of employees in the factory or plant. Over and over again we quite unconsciously use a word or a phrase to mean something entirely different from the physical object which the word or phrase designates.

A symbol, therefore, is something that stands for or represents or recalls something else – not by exact resemblance, but by suggestion or association of thought. Thus the head stands for knowledge and intellectual capacity. When we say that a man 'has a good head', we mean that he thinks and reasons; he uses his intellect instead of allowing his actions to be controlled by passion or prejudice or partisanship. Plainly, when we make that statement about a man, we do not refer to his physical head, but to his ability to use his intellect to arrive at valid conclusions based on fact and evidence.

Again, take an old-fashioned hour-glass. It is a wrought piece of glass so constructed that it is thin in the middle to allow the grains of sand to pass slowly from one chamber to the other. To the instructed Mason, and indeed to all thinking people, the hour-glass symbolises the passage of time, slow, but sure and relentless. 'I consider Time as an immense ocean', wrote Addison.

> See how the generations pass
> Like sand through Heaven's hour-glass.

As our final illustration of how physical objects become symbols, let us consider the apron which the Mason wears. Physically it is a piece of cloth or lambskin of a certain shape and design. To every Mason, however, it symbolises that purity of life and rectitude of conduct which characterise the true Mason.

Freemasonry, like nature, uses the language of symbols in its teaching. 'Nature speaks in symbols and signs', wrote Whittier. Thomas Carlyle, the English essayist, has a thought provoking paragraph in *Sartor Resartus*, which we shall do well to read and ponder.

> By Symbols is man guided and commanded, made happy, made wretched. He everywhere finds himself encompassed with symbols, recognised as such or not recognised. The Universe is but one vast Symbol of God. Nay, what is man himself but a Symbol of God? Is not all that he does symbolical – a revelation to sense of the mystic God-given force that is in him – a Gospel of Freedom, which he, the Messiah of Nature, preaches, as he can, by word and act? Not a Hut he builds but is the visible embodiment of a Thought; but bears visible record of invisible things; but is, in the transcendental sense, symbolical as well as real.

Let us attend also to that great masonic thinker and philosopher, Albert Pike.

Masonry still follows the ancient manner of teaching. Her symbols are the instructions she gives; and the lectures are often but partial and insufficient one-sided endeavours to interpret those symbols. He who would become an accomplished Mason must not be content merely to hear or even to understand the lectures, but must, aided by them, and they having as it were marked out the way for him, study, interpret, and develop the symbols for himself.

Only as we get deeply embedded into our minds and hearts that attitude set out in Pike's inspiring words can we profit from our study of Masonic symbolism.

I have long since concluded that nothing is gained by attempting to make fine distinctions in the use of the words symbol and emblem. For all practical Masonic purposes, an emblem may be a symbol, and a symbol may be an emblem. A cross consisted originally of two wooden pieces – the shorter piece nailed transversely on the longer piece. Symbolically the cross is the emblem or symbol of suffering; it is also the emblem or symbol of Christianity. In the same way the dove is the emblem or symbol of peace; white is the emblem or symbol of purity; black is the emblem or symbol of mourning.

An allegory is a narrative in which certain teaching is conveyed symbolically. John Bunyan's *Pilgrim's Progress* is an extended allegory. Its characters and events are pure fiction – the outcome of Bunyan's vivid imagination. Published in 1678, *Pilgrim's Progress* remains one of the classics of the English language. The irresistible charm of the book, as Lord Macaulay wrote, gratifies the imagination of the reader, but nevertheless leaves in his mind a sentiment of reverence for God and of sympathy for man. The story 'moves'. Its purpose, however, is by no means merely to tell an imaginative story; on the contrary, it succeeds marvellously in setting forth a teaching about the Christian way of life and its ultimate triumph.

A parable is like an allegory, but is specifically related to a religious or moral subject. Over and over again the Master of Men used parables to drive home the truths of his teaching. The parable of the Good Samaritan, for example, teaches many ramifications of truth – the evil of selfishness, the essential brotherhood of all men, the worth of generous impulse and actions, the love of God for erring man – to mention but a few.

As we study the emblems, the symbols, and the allegories of freemasonry we ought to keep in mind two basic principles of interpretation. Firstly, there is no 'authorised' interpretation of a masonic symbol. In this respect freemasonry is like Protestantism. The essence of the reformed faith is the right of individual interpretation. Protestantism rejects the idea that any man's statements are infallible. Secondly that every interpretation of a symbol must be consistent with the meaning – the genius – of freemasonry; that is to say, the meaning we draw from a symbol must be in accord with what freemasonry is. Unless we observe that principle of interpretation in our study and thinking, we can easily go off into all kinds of wild speculation, so that anything can mean anything. That kind of speculation, because it fails to take into account the history and philosophy of freemasonry, may lead to all kinds of excesses.

Another danger to be avoided in the study of masonic symbolism is the human tendency to make interpretations that are trivial and ordinary. Albert Pike has this to say: 'To translate the symbols into the trivial and commonplace is the blunder of mediocrity'. Some blunders of that kind were made by the makers of our Monitors in days gone by – blunders that are perpetuated to this day. It is the kind of blundering which lies at the back of a statement made in the 25 July 1949 issue of *Time* magazine in an article entitled, 'The World of Hiram Abiff'. We read, 'Although Masonry's ritual is private, it contains no dreadful secret'. That statement is entirely correct. Then the article goes on to say, 'Its symbolism is commonplace (e.g. the trowel cements men in brotherly love; the white lambskin apron is for innocence)'. The whole article is pervaded by a tongue-in-cheek attitude.

Of course, if we are content to do commonplace and trivial thinking then, naturally enough, our interpretation of the Masonic emblems and symbols and allegories will be commonplace and trivial too. What lies on the surface is often of minor value. You have to dig, and dig deep, for real treasures;

something that is obviously beyond the comprehension of anybody who superciliously writes that the symbolism of freemasonry is 'commonplace'.

There is no denying the fact it is often difficult to attach adequate meanings to some Masonic symbols. The symbolism of freemasonry is not an easy subject. There has been a vast deal of rubbish written on Masonic symbolism. It has been, as an English Masonic scholar wrote, 'the happy hunting ground for those who, guided by no system or rule, love to allow their fancies and imagination to run wild.' Interpretations are given which have no other foundation than the disordered brain of the writer. The thoughtful Masonic writer avoids going out on a limb of fanciful speculation.

What we need to get firmly fixed in our minds is this basic fact. The symbolism of freemasonry is the really important and significant aspect of the Craft. Let us attend to what brother Oliver Day Street says in his book, *Symbolism of the Three Degrees*.

> It may be asserted in the broadest terms that the Mason who knows nothing of our symbolism knows little of Freemasonry. He may be able to repeat every line of the ritual without an error; and yet, if he does not understand the meaning of the ceremonies, the signs, the words, the emblems, and the figures, he is an ignoramus Masonically. It is distressing to witness how much time and labour are spent in memorising 'the Work' and how little in ascertaining what it all means.

Now, neither brother Street nor any other right-thinking Mason underrates for one minute the importance of letter perfect rendition of the ritual. The ritual is the vehicle by which Masonic lessons are conveyed. Any Mason who has any part of the rendition of any Masonic Body ought to do the work for which he is responsible in such a way as to impress the candidate or candidates with the beauty, the moving power of it all. That impression, be it said, can be made only when the ritualist himself understands the meaning that lies imbedded in the sentences he is repeating.

So far we have been thinking about the nature of Masonic

symbolisms. As is so often the case, Albert Pike sums up for us the right attitude. 'Every symbol', he writes, 'is a religious teacher, the mute teacher also of morals and philosophy. It is in its ancient symbols and in the knowledge of their true meaning that the pre-eminence of freemasonry over all other orders consists.' 'Each symbol', he concludes 'is the embodiment of some great, old, rare truth.'

It is that attitude of searching for the meaning of the symbols, the emblems, and the allegories of freemasonry that should always permeate our study of Masonic symbolism. We thus avoid idle speculation on the one hand, and trivial and commonplace thinking on the other hand.

The very word Masonry is itself symbolical. When we use the word masonry (with a small m), we refer to the actual or literal work of a builder in stone or brick, a worker who is referred to as a mason (or stonemason), just as workers in other trades are called carpenters or plumbers or glaziers.

The tools of a mason fall into five groups; saws, hammers and mallets, chisels, setting tools, and hoisting appliances. These literal tools go far back in the history of mankind. To this day it remains a mystery how the ancient builders in Egypt and India, for example, were able to quarry and raise to great heights above the ground, blocks which were often seven or eight hundred tons in weight. Modern science, of course, has given us mechanical hoisting appliances. They play an indispensable part in construction work in our time.

Some aspects of the modern trade of masonry are taught in vocational schools. For the most part, however, it is a trade that is learned 'on the job'. Young men become apprentices in the trade of masonry in its various fields; they get their training under skilled workmen. Eventually they, too, become master masons in the operative sense.

Now, it is perfectly plain that Masonry (spelled with a capital M) is something entirely different from the trade we have just been thinking about. It is also obvious that a man whom we call a Mason (again spelled with a capital M) does not necessarily have any association with, or know anything about, masonry.

A great deal of time and much laborious scholarship have

been expended in the effort to determine the derivation of the word masonry. There is a Latin word *massa*, which means a club or society. One of the meanings of our English word mass (derived from *massa*) is a quantity of matter or an aggregation of things or people united into one body. Thus we speak of a mass of material or a mass meeting. We also use the word to refer to the act of collecting into a body. We speak, for example, about a massed choir. We say that a man amasses a fortune.

In all the variation of the word masonry down through the centuries, we always find in it the idea of bringing together, of unity. Much of the work of the operative mason, of course, consists of bringing together the various materials he uses. The goal which he has before him is the formation of a compact mass or structure of some kind. 'The mason masses', as an English Masonic scholar has said, 'and the work he does is masonry'.

So much for the meaning of the word masonry. We now leave the subject of literal building in order to think about figurative or symbolical building. Until we get firmly fixed in our minds and hearts the fundamental fact that Masonry is character building, we handicap ourselves in the use we make of Masonry. For, be it said, Masonry is a science, a philosophy, a way of living. Furthermore, Masonry is wider than a Masonic lodge and deeper than any Masonic ritual. The elements of Masonry are expressed through the ritual as rendered in a lodge, but the ritual is but the bare bones.

Later in this paper we shall look at the symbolism wrapped up in the word Lodge. Right here we need to emphasise to ourselves the basic fact that Masonry in its symbolical meaning – the only meaning that really matters – carries with it the idea of building – of erecting a structure – of massing together. But that building and that structure and that massing have nothing whatever to do with stone or mortar. Men who are true Masons are constantly engaged in the building of character – their own character and the character of others, Masonry, then, is moral building. That building is done according to a plan.

The best-known statement about Masonry comes down to us from the eighteenth century: 'Masonry is a system of Morality, veiled in Allegory and illustrated by Symbols'. We cannot rightly say that this statement is a definition of Masonry. It is at best an aphorism – and not a true aphorism at that. As a Masonic writer has said, 'The morality of Freemasonry is not veiled at all, but is set forth in quite clear English in the ritual, although it is illustrated by symbols'.

Again we read that Masonry is a 'progressive science'. But, as the writer whom we have just quoted goes on to say, 'it is not a science; and if it is progressive, then a large segment of the Craft is wrong in thinking it quite fixed and permanent in its doctrine'.

Still, we can truly say that in a real sense Masonry is first of all a system. It is something planned and organised. Its parts fit together. It is not something haphazard and unsystematic. Second, it is certainly a system of morality, which means the doctrine of right and wrong in human thinking and acting. Often we attach too narrow a meaning to the words morality and immorality. Whatever action is in accord with truth and right and honour is moral; whatever is untrue, unrighteous, and dishonest is immoral. Too often we think of the word immoral in a limited sense as meaning unchaste or promiscuous.

The use of the word veiled in the statement quoted is unfortunate. The truth is that what Masonry seeks to teach is not veiled, but perfectly open to the understanding of the thoughtful Mason. The lessons which Masonry seeks to impress on the minds and hearts of Masons are often revealed (not veiled) in allegories and illustrated by symbols.

In its essence Masonry is an elaborate allegory of life – from birth through youth and maturity to old age and death, and beyond death to immortality. Whenever we think or talk about the literal aspects of the ritual, therefore, we ought to understand clearly that behind the words and sentences which we hear lie profound allegorical and symbolical meanings.

Again we can profit by Albert Pike's thinking. 'We build slowly. Therefore, faint not, nor be weary in well-doing.

Be not discouraged at men's apathy, nor disgusted with their follies, nor tired of their indifference. Care not for returns and results; but see only what there is to do and do it, leaving the results to God'.

Much of the symbolism of modern Masonry goes far back in time. In order to understand the essential meaning of Masonic symbols, therefore, we need to know something about the practices that were in vogue among the Cathedral Builders of the Middle Ages who were, in a sense, the progenitors of the Craft as we know it today. We need, therefore, to think about the idea of symbolical building as that idea has come down to us from the far past.

The conception of symbolical building has been voiced by sages and prophets and poets in all ages. St Paul referred to himself as a 'master builder'. Over and over again in the early Christian writings we find references to building on foundations and to a building fitly framed together. We may recall, too, the stanza from Longfellow's poem, *The Builders*

> In the elder days of Art,
>   Builders wrought with greatest care
> Each minute and unseen part;
>   For the Gods see everywhere.

Many of us, too, will remember from our school days the stanza from *The Chambered Nautilus* by Oliver Wendell Holmes

> Build thee more stately mansions, O my soul,
> As the swift seasons roll.
> Leave thy low-vaulted Past!
> Let each new temple, nobler than the last,
> Shut thee from heaven with a dome more vast,
> Till thou at length art free,
> Leaving thine outgrown shell by life's unresting sea.

Let us meditate also on the profound truth that Edwin Markham, Master Mason and the author of *The Man with the Hoe*, put into this question and its answer

> Why build these cities glorious
> If man unbuilded goes?
> In vain we build the world unless
> The builder also grows.

A thousand comparable utterances by the thinkers of the past could easily be adduced. The idea of building character is a part of human folklore.

The basic purpose of freemasonry is to build individual character. It does not build a religious organisation or a political party. It works in and through individual Masons. It can do its proper share in building a better world only as its tenets and principles are built into the character, the thinking, and the acting of you and me and all other Masons. To the extent that we think of freemasonry exclusively as a ritual, as a social organisation, or even as a fraternity, to that extent also we lose sight of the real meaning of freemasonry.

Building character is something that goes on throughout life. No Mason ever comes to the point when he can say that he has obtained from Masonry everything it has to offer. The holding of offices in the Masonic fraternity is not necessarily growth in freemasonry any more than a perfect knowledge of the ritual necessarily means that character has been built. To know what is right does not at all mean that a man will do what is right. It is the easiest thing in the world to confuse the externals with the internal truths of freemasonry.

Now that we have looked briefly at the fundamental facts about Symbolic Masonry – namely, that it is intended to exemplify the building of character – let us look at the symbolism wrapped up in the word Lodge.

When the Operative Masons of the Middle Ages were engaged to build a Cathedral, their first step was to erect temporary huts around or near the place where the Cathedral was to be erected. Those huts or sheds were places where the workmen ate and slept – where they lived (and commingled) when they were not engaged in actual building. In Germany those huts were called Hutten; in England they were referred to as Lodges.

The word Lodge comes from an old Anglo-Saxon word

which means to dwell. When Speculative Masonry gained control of Operative Masonry in the early eighteenth century, the word Lodge was naturally carried over into Masonic language to designate the place where Masons congregated or met together. The more exact term for this meaning of the word is Lodge-room. Properly speaking, a Lodge is an organised body of Masons who come together for labour or business. The word is specifically associated with Symbolic Masonry, just as Chapter is associated with Capitular Masonry and Council with Cryptic Masonry. The term Blue Lodge, by the way, is Masonic slang.

'The central motor-idea in the old Operative Lodge', writes Brother A. S. McBride in his thought-provoking book, *Speculative Masonry,*

> was the building of a sacred structure. In the same way, but symbolically, the motor-idea of the Speculative Lodge is the building of a sacred structure in accordance with the plan of life laid down by the Great Architect. The Symbols of the outer world – the insignia of rank, the sword of power, and the purse of wealth – are laid aside. . . . The True Mason Lodge provides an environment for the development of the nobler nature of man, for the formation or building up of high character. Character is built of the thoughts which we allow to grow and multiply in our minds. . . . It is the workshop wherein the souls of men may be shaped, moulded, and made fit for the Great Ideal Temple. Where, we cry, is there neutral ground where all conflicting elements may be hushed to peace, and where good men of all conditions, creeds, and colours may meet in the bonds of Brotherhood? There is only one spot on earth we know of that fulfils this condition, and that is here in the Mason Lodge. Here all may meet together on a common level as children of the One Great Father, members of the same human family, and brethren of the same mystic tie.

The antiquity of Masonic symbolism is further attested by the expression 'oblong square'. To our modern way of thinking, there is no such thing as an oblong square. We think of a square as a figure with four sides of equal length. In ancient times, however, square meant simply right-angled. There were two kinds of squares – the perfect square, in which the four sides are equal in length, and the oblong square, in which two of the parallel sides – each equal in length – are longer than the other two sides of identical length. Each perfect square and each oblong square, of course, has four right angles.

Men in ancient times thought of the world as being an 'oblong' square. Many of the buildings they erected – especially places of worship – were constructed in the form of 'oblong' squares. The ritual thus connects modern Speculative Masonry with the thinking and the building practices of our ancient Operative Brethren.

Just as the world includes high hills and low vales, so in a Masonic Lodge there are to be found men of all intellectual backgrounds. In a Masonic Lodge, however, they all meet on the level of their common humanity.

One of the heart-warming facts about freemasonry is that its purpose is always to unite – never to separate; always to bring together, never to keep apart. In the Lodge are men of many minds, of all religions, of all levels of education, of all vocations, and of all degrees of wealth and poverty. In the Masonic Lodge those men of different backgrounds and various stations in life can and do unite in a faith that needs no dogma or creed.

The world about us is governed by the laws of nature and nature's God. The world of freemasonry, too, has its laws, its Constitutions, its Ancient Landmarks. 'A Mason is obliged by his tenure to obey the moral Law'. So reads the first sentence of the first Charge of the Constitutions of 1723. Those Constitutions stand in the same relation to freemasonry that the Constitution of the United States stands to our country. In that same Charge there is set out the basic law governing Masonic fellowship.

> Though in ancient times Masons were charged in every country to be of the religion of that country or nation, whatever it was, yet now 'tis thought more expedient only to oblige them to that religion in which all men agree, leaving their particular opinions to themselves; that is, to be good men and true, or men of honour and honesty, by whatever denominations or persuasions they may be

distinguished; whereby Masonry becomes the centre of union and the means of conciliating true friendship among persons who must have remained at a perpetual distance.

In the world of freemasonry there is agreement on those underlying moral principles to which all right-thinking men subscribe. In that world a Mason's religious affiliation is not a factor. It is required of him only that he join with his brethren in a sincere belief in the God who rules heaven and earth; that he uphold the moral law in all its applications and implications; that he regard each brother for what he is as a man and a Mason without reference to this status in the outer world.

Just as the Lodge symbolises the world, so the Mason symbolises man – the human race. Initiation represents the introduction of the individual into the Masonic world. In the Ancient Mysteries the initiatory rites were regarded as a symbol of birth. That same symbolism prevails in freemasonry. The least important view of initiation is to consider it merely as a method of admitting men to membership in the fraternity.

Perhaps all that we have been saying can be summarised in this statement: Masons are building character in the world of Masonry. That building is carried on by each Mason working in co-operation with other Masons. It is character building that goes on in a sphere that is actuated and pervaded by high and noble motives, by a common faith in God, by a belief in the dignity of human personality, by a sympathetic understanding and appreciation of the honest convictions of others. I have tried to put that sympathetic understanding which should characterise Masonic fellowship into a little poem which I call 'The Fraternal Tie'.

> What faith my Brothers hold in sacred trust
>   That faith to me is sacred too.
> I count all honest faith as true and just,
>   And thus I gain a wider view.
> In Masonry the walls are broken down,
>   Free thought and conscience there prevail,
> Respect, goodwill, and understanding crown
>   The Lodge with joys that never fail.

> The faith we hold in common far transcends
> The things and doctrines that divide.
> Fraternal feeling makes us brothers, friends –
> A tie that stretches far and wide.
> Of sects and parties we have naught to teach.
> We hold the Fatherhood of God,
> The Brotherhood of Man, the Soul's far reach.
> Hold fast these truths as on you plod.

Sympathy – feeling with – is the distinguishing characteristic of the true Mason. He is genuine, sympathetic and truly understanding in his attitude, not merely tolerant. Tolerance carries with it the idea of patronising others by allowing them to think as they wish. It puts the emphasis on the ego when the emphasis should be on others. 'Live and help live' expresses the true Masonic attitude rather than 'Live and let live'.

Dr Mackay has admirably summed up for us the symbolism which is associated with the Lodge itself. He tells us that a Lodge, when it is duly opened, is a symbol of the world. 'Its covering is like the world's, a sky or Clouded Canopy, to reach which, as the abode of those who do the will of the Grand Architect, it is furnished with the theological ladder that reaches from earth to heaven. It is illuminated, as is the world, by the refulgent rays of the sun, symbolically represented in his rising in the East, his meridian height in the South, and his setting in the West; and, lastly, its very form a long quadrangle or oblong square, is in reference to the early tradition that such was the shape of the inhabited world.'

When we sit in a Masonic Lodge, therefore, it is the symbolism with which it is freighted that ought to occupy our minds. The Lodge is, as Dr Joseph Fort Newton has beautifully said, 'both a place of quiet and purity and a method by which work may be carried on. Sect and party, creed and strife are excluded. Not out of the world, but separate from it, close tyled in a chamber of moral imagery and in the fellowship of men seeking the good life, we may learn what life is and how to live it'.

The harmony of God's world is often broken by the evil passions of men. In the world of freemasonry, which is the

Lodge, hate, envy, and evil have no place. There is that world of wisdom, strength, and beauty, we are taught the Faith that makes us men. 'Where in all the world', asks Dr Newton, 'is there another such shrine of peace and beauty where men of all ranks, creeds, and conditions are drawn together as brothers of the mystic tie, dedicated and devoted to the best life?'

No matter how humble a Masonic Lodge may be in its situation or in its appointments, the thoughtful Mason still sees in it the symbolism which is its basic characteristic. Besides the home and the House of God, there is no other place in all the world where thoughtful men may better learn what life is and what it is meant to be.

7

SOME NOTES ON THE MARK DEGREE

F. E. Gould

THE FOLLOWING PAPER was one of several on the subject of the Mark Degree that is has been my privilege and pleasure to deliver to the Western District Mark Master Masons' Association. It was delivered on 29 November 1955.

Whilst it does not profess to be more than 'Some Notes on the Mark Degree', I have, I trust, given some useful information and brought together some historical data respecting the degree as applied to the jurisdictions of Scotland, England and Ireland.

With regard to the origin of the English Grand Lodge of Mark Master Masons, I have quoted in full the historical introduction which appeared in the constitutions of the Mark Master Masons of 1864, for I do not think that this has been reprinted in extenso in any book or pamphlet on the degree since that date.

Many masons, although willing, and indeed anxious to learn something more of the nature of the Institution into which they have been introduced, and the meaning of the ceremonies through which they have passed, are very often unable, from the want of time needed for research, inability to locate suitable material to assist them, or lack the means to indulge their laudable curiosity. Further, because of the belief held by many brethren that it is only the degrees of EA, FC, MM and RA that constitute the essential structure, the beautiful and impressive ceremony of Mark Masonry is either ignored or at best considered as a degree to be bestowed upon those only who have the time and inclination to receive it.

So essentially is Mark Masonry a connecting link between Craft and Royal Arch that it behoves those who have hitherto given little thought to the derivation of masonic ceremonies to examine its historical antiquity.

In its earlier form the degree was bestowed between that of fellow Craft and MM and was bound up both historically and ritually with those degrees, as a study of the degree as worked in Scotland from the earliest times will show. As Brother J. A. Grantham is his *Introduction to Mark Masonry* says: 'The traditions rather than the number of degrees in the early days of organised freemasonry should be the main concern of the student seeking enlightenment on those parts of masonry lying beyond what is usually designated Craft'.

In making this paper available to others beyond my brethren of the Western District Mark Masters' Association, who gave it such a good reception, I venture to hope that its appearance in print will stimulate interest, research, and study of this time-honoured degree.

The importance of the Mark Degree as a connecting link with the operative Masons' customs and traditions prior to the formation of the premier Grand Lodge is not always fully appreciated, particularly by those freemasons under the obedience of the English Rite and Constitution. Perhaps this can be attributed to the fact that at the Union of the two rival Grand Lodges – the Antients and the Moderns, in 1813 – it was laid down that Pure Antient Masonry consists of three degrees, including the Holy Royal Arch.

Let it be remembered that it was only in the spirit of compromise that the Moderns admitted that the Royal Arch was part and parcel of speculative freemasonry and that whereas it was always considered by the 'Antients' as an essential ceremony, not all lodges under the 'Moderns' had worked that degree up to the time of the Union.

It must not be hastily assumed, however, that the Articles of

Union, adopted in 1813 by the United Grand Lodge, limited masonic activities to no more than the working of the degrees mentioned. A careful reading of Article II gives a far different understanding, for after enumerating the degrees of EA, FC, MM, including the Supreme Order of the Holy Royal Arch, it goes on to say, 'But this article is not intended to prevent any Lodge or Chapter from holding a meeting in any degree of the Orders of Chivalry, according to the Constitution of the said Orders.'

The important point is that whilst it was realised that lodges had worked and would continue to work the Mark degree, a degree that had, in common with the craft degrees gone through various forms and changes, responsibility for its organisation was unfortunately not accepted by the United Grand Lodge.

In Scotland and Ireland the position was different as we find by studying the records and constitutions of these jurisdictions. Whilst masonic historians may differ as to the precise date at which the Mark *as a degree* can be established there can be no doubt whatsoever that the use of Marks by operative masons goes back into the dim past.

To trace these Marks through the centuries, throughout the civilised world, and attempt to classify them is not my purpose, though I shall refer later to some of them.

Brother Mackey says,

> As a degree of freemasonry, in the sense which we give to the word 'degree' the system of Mark Freemasonry was wholly unknown to the Operative Freemasons of the Middle Ages. . . . In Germany every Apprentice who had served his time, on being admitted as a Fellow Craft received a Mark, which was to be his unchangeably during his life.
>
> The giving of this mark of distinction was generally accompanied by a banquet, furnished to a certain extent at the expense of the Lodge which admitted him. But there is not the least allusion in any document extant to the fact that the bestowal of the Mark was accompanied by any secret ceremonies which would give it the slightest resemblance to a degree.

But, says Mackey:

The very instinct of a group of persons engaged in a serious and important ceremony, approving of a certain Mark which was to be preserved for life by the one receiving it and having a use that meant much to everyone in the trade, must have invited and probably suggested a method or ritual to impress upon all present the fullest meaning and purpose of their engagements one to another.

If this did not result in a typical and appropriate ceremony the case would be exceptional and opposed to all our experience.

With the era of the 'Acception' and development of speculative masonry, there is not doubt that many of the operative masons who had joined forces with the non-operatives took advantage of the opportunity presented to them by their association to suggest a ritualistic formula which would enshrine forever the traditions of centuries of operative craft legends and customs.

One feels that long before the idea of a Grand Lodge had been mooted, much less come into being, the operatives amongst the speculatives were in the main the instigators in formulating special ceremonies which had for their object the incorporation of operative craft customs, legends, traditions, and other aspects.

Thus some commemoration in ritualist form of the customs and use of Marks on stones by operative masons especially those used in the building of Churches, Abbeys and Cathedrals dedicated to Christian service would be provided by a deeply significant spiritual aim adding beauty and dignity to the lessons submitted.

Brother Waite, referring to Christian allusions in the Mark Degree, says,

> It takes us back also to that earlier state of masonry, the ante-Grand Lodge period, when Rituals such as they were – were not memorials of Judaistic Deism. There is none which bears comparison with it for the wealth and significance of its Christian allusions and implicits. The counsel throughout is to become so built up within that we shall be in fine meet 'for his habitation' – that is to say, for the Divine Indwelling. This is the kind of building and this the Operative Masonry. I carry no brief for maintaining

that any Masonic Ritual is altogether perfect in its parts or unreservedly honourable to its builders, but those who have followed the story of the Mystic stone which is now Lapis reprobatus, now caput anguli, now set in its place to complete the Arch of Doctrine, now torn therefrom in quest of the Lost Word, will know that the ceremony of Advancement in the Mark Degree deserves to be put in its proper place with due pomp and worship. As to those who ruled it out in the past from the narrow scheme of things which they called Masonry, I need say only that it possessed merits to them unknown.

What we now know as the Mark Degree has been evolved from a number of unrelated grades, portions of which were from time to time grafted on to one of the forms of what may be called Key Stone Mark Masonry as we have it today. These degrees included Mark Man, Mark Master, link and Chain, Fugitive Mark, Christian Mark, Cain's Mark, Travelling Mark, and others.

In England, according to the earliest reference traced and to which I shall later make reference, there were two distinctive forms – Mark Masons and Mark Masters – and in these forms it complied with that of the Scottish working, where the business of the Mark Man antecedes that of the Master.

That which prevails under the obedience of the Grand Mark Lodge of England and Wales appears to be inconsistent for, as Brother Waite says, it 'stultifies the symbolical procedure by its violence to the logic of things, reversing as it does the position of the two points, so that the candidate is compelled to go back on the step which he has taken, as if renouncing the status which he has reached, though it has received official recognition. . . . I am confident that [the Scottish] is the earlier arrangement and belongs to the original form, more especially as it is obviously that which obtained in the Chapter of Friendship [Portsmouth] in 1769.'

What brother Waite was pointing out is that the business of Mark Man anteceded that of Mark Master and that the old Scottish working was the more consistent procedure.

Brother Mackenzie in the prefatory remarks to his *Mark Work* says,

At a certain point of the work it is by no means unlikely that the main incident of the Mark Degree might have taken place, as the distance from the Quarries of hewn stone was too considerable, and the stations of the officers too perfectly defined, to allow of an immediate correction of any supposed offence. The worst that it is possible to suggest to a Candidate for the Mark Masters' Degree, is that he had managed to bring up a piece of work unsuitable for the present requirements of the building, and this, coming out of its ordinary series, would lead to his temporary embarrassment. Then the offering being further disdained, he would be free to linger about, and receive his wages as he supposed, which would finally produce the catastrophe, and thus give rise to the peculiar degree of Mark Master Mason.

This, however, was not always so: the Degree was, *in its origin, far more sensible*. The Mark Man brought his 'fair stone and square stone' and received his wages for it; and it was only because the peculiarly shaped stone was brought up that the Mark Master's Degree was originated.

At any rate, looking at the history of the Degree, it is impossible to doubt that such a fact led to the Degree being founded. But we have now only to deal with matters as they exist. The Mark Man's Degree is absorbed, and the Mark Master's Degree maintained. There never has been a doubt that Mark Men had their several marks, as the whole history of architecture shows beyond question.

With regard to the Antiquity of Mark Masonry, we have the statement of the masonic historian, the RW Brother W. J. Hughan, who in the Introduction to a 'Collection of Articles on Mark Masonry', reprinted from *The Freemason*, which originally appeared in May and June, 1905, says,

> The antiquity of Mark Masonry cannot be doubted, operatively considered; and even speculatively, it has enjoyed special prominence for centuries; records of the custom [of recording distinctive marks] being followed by speculative Brethren, according to existing records, dating back to 1600, in which year, on the 8th day of June 'Ye principal warden and cheif maister of maissons, Wm. Schaw, maister of werk to ye Kingis maistie' met members of the Lodge of Edinburgh [now No 1] at Holyrood House, at which meeting the Laird of Auchinleck was present, and attested the minutes of the assembly by his mark, as did the operatives, in accordance with the Schaw Statutes of Dec. 28th, 1598, which

provided 'That the day of ressanyng [receiving] of the said fallow of craft or maister be ord'lie buikit and his name and mark insert in the said buik'. The theoretical [or non-operative] Masons selected their marks just as the operatives did, during the seventeenth century, is abundantly manifest by an examination of the old Scottish Records of that period.

Article 13 of the oft-quoted *Schaw Statutes* of 1598 provides the foundation on which has been erected the edifice of Mark Masonry. This article recites that no Master or Fellow Craft is to be received or admitted except in the presence of six Masters (who must include the Warden of the lodge) and two Entered Apprentices. The date of admission must be entered in the book, and the candidate's name and mark inserted in that book.

It will be seen that the use of a 'Mark' was a necessity for every brother of a Scottish lodge in the seventeenth century. A register of such Marks was kept with the greatest regularity, probably because Scottish lodges retained their operative character long after English lodges had become purely speculative. Theoretical masons, however, selected a Mark in exactly the same way, as for example in the Lodge of Aberdeen.

Here we find one of the most noteworthy instances out of many, for in the Mark Book of that Lodge (now No 1 ter) which was started in AD 1670 we have the signatures of forty-nine members at that date, all of whom but two have their marks inserted opposite their names.

The Master of the 'Honourable Lodge of Aberdeen' in 1670 was Harrie Elphinstone, Tutor of Airth and Collector of the King's Customs, and only a fourth part of the members were operative masons, the roll of brethren including the Earl of Findlater, the Earl of Dumferline, Lord Pitsligo, the 'Earle of Errole', a Professor of Mathematics, several Ministers, Doctors and other professional men, and Tradesmen, such as Wrights (or Carpenters), Slaiters, Glaziers, etc.

The Mark Degree in Scotland

It is evident that in Scotland from somewhere about the

1760s the ceremonies in connection with the Mark as a Degree was in two parts and was designed to be complementary to that of Fellow Craft: the first part being that of Mark Man and the second part for those who had reached the degree of Master and was in this form a natural sequence. Dr Oliver in his writings points out that in England before the 'Union' in 1813 the degree was practised by many lodges as an integral part of the Fellow Craft.

Mackey says:

> In Scotland, after the transition of Operative into Speculative Freemasonry, the Mark Degree was worked originally by a few Lodges under their craft warrant, and it was then conferred as an addition or part of the Fellow Craft degree. This was done as late as 1860 by a Lodge at Glasgow. This action, however, attracted the notice of the Grand Chapter and, having in conference with the Grand Lodge thoroughly investigated the subject, the following report was made. As giving a summary of the rise and progress of the degree in Scotland, and of the changes of position to which it was subjected, this report is well worthy of quotation. It was unanimously agreed by the Committee of Conference that what is generally known under the name of the Mark Masters' degree was wrought by the Operative Lodges of St John's Masonry in connection with the Fellow Craft degree before the institution of the Grand Lodge of Scotland [*ie* prior to 1736].
>
> [Here I would point out that by St John's Masonry is meant the three symbolic degrees of EA, FC AND MM.]
>
> That since that date it has continued to be wrought in the Old Operative Lodges, but in what may be called the Speculative Lodges it was never worked at all – or, at all events, only in a few. That this degree being, with the exception of the Old Operative Lodges above mentioned, entirely abandoned by the Lodges of St John's Masonry, the Supreme Grand Royal Arch Chapter assumed the Management of it as the Fourth Degree of Masonry in order to complete the instruction of their candidates in the preliminary degrees before admitting them to the Royal Arch. And, finally, that this degree, whether viewed as a second part of the Fellow Craft degree or as a separate degree, has never been recognised or worked in England, Ireland, or the Continent, or in America, as a part of St John's Masonry.

In Scotland there is now no distinction between Mark Man and Mark Master; the former term is unknown. The Early Grand Scottish Rite (which came to an end some forty-odd years ago) made a distinction between them. Under this Rite a Mark Man came below the Master Mason and the Mark Master came after, the Master Mason's Degree thus coming between the two Mark Degrees.

In Scotland there is no recognised or authorised ritual for any of the degrees, and each lodge, so long as it gives essentials, can work as it pleases. In some Chapters the ritual worked is practically identical with the English version, the chief difference being a much longer lecture to the candidate after his obligation; this being, however, an extension rather than a variation of that given in English Mark lodges.

Mark Masonry in Scotland is under the jurisdiction of both Grand Chapter and Grand Lodge. Every lodge warranted by Grand Lodge is empowered to work the Mark and it is so worked universally throughout Scotland. The large majority of Scottish Masons now take the Mark from the lodge and not from the chapter, but both jurisdictions work in perfect amity in this respect and recognise the Mark Masons made by either.

In Scotland a Brother must be a Mark Mason before he can be exalted into the degree of the Royal Arch.

His Scottish Royal Arch Certificate implies that he has received the degree of Mark Mason and should be accepted as evidence thereof. When a Royal Arch Mason is appointed 'Z' he receives the Mark Installed Degree.

An English Royal Arch Mason is recognised in Scotland but not admitted to a Chapter until after Passing the Veils.

A Scottish Royal Arch Mason, who has served the office of First Principal, must have been installed into the Chair of a Mark Lodge previously.

Earliest known Scottish Minute: Dumfries, 1770

As distinct from the registering of Marks, which, as we have seen, was a very much earlier custom in Scotland, the earliest known Scottish minute which refers to the *Mark Degree* comes from Dumfriesshire.

The Journeymen Lodge of Dumfries, now known as the Thistle Lodge, No 62 (SC) constituted on 6 June 1753 has records which show that the Royal Arch, and all it implied, was practised at a very early date. Unfortunately, several pages of the original minute book have been destroyed, but at the end of the book is a page headed 'Record of Royal Arch Masons, and their passing to that', and the first name on the list is entered as 9 November 1756. The steps comprising 'passing to that' – the Royal Arch – are made evident in the first surviving minute relative to ultra-Craft Degrees. The relative minute of 8 October 1770 records the 'elevation of a brother to the Degree of Royal Arch Mason', and sets out a form of certificate as follows:

> In the beginning was the Word, and the Light shined in darkness, and the darkness comprehended it not. The bearer hereof . . . came to us well recommended, of good report, and free from public scandal. In consequence, we the Master, etc., of the ―――― hereby certify and attest to all men enlightened that the said worshipful brother, after having been examined and found duly qualified as an Entered Apprentice, Fellow Craft, Master, and *Mark Master Mason*, was by us elected Master of the Chair, and then by us elevated to the Sublime Degree of Excellent, Super-Excellent, and Royal Arch Mason and as such we do hereby recommend him. [Etc.]
>
> [*Note* – This extract is from the Appendix, *Early Royal Arch Masonry in Annan*, by J. Smith, p 81, which is appended to D. A. Knox, *History of Lodge Caledonian, No 238, Annan*, published in 1911.]

The Mark Master Degree was apparently conferred according to the sequence as now considered correct, *ie* following that of Master Mason. The Master of the Chair was the so-called Constructive Chair Degree.

Brother Grantham, in his *Introduction to Mark Masonry*, p 35 of the 1934 edition, observes:

> This minute is not the record of an innovation. The Lodge was competent to form itself into what is now termed a Royal Arch Chapter, and to confer the Royal Arch Degrees, and had obviously been in the habit of doing so, as both the wording of this Minute and the 'Record of Royal Arch Masons' indicate.

The loss of the earlier minutes [1753 to ? September 1770] is to be regretted, for they may well have afforded a mention of Mark Masonry predating that of the Portsmouth Chapter of Friendship of September 1769, to which I shall refer shortly.

Another early reference to the Mark Degree in Scotland is mentioned by Brother Hughan in his introduction to Wm Logan's *History of Freemasonry in the City of Durham.* This refers to St John's Operative Lodge, Banff, now No 92(SC). A more detailed account appeared in the *Scottish Freemason,* July 1895, where a minute of this lodge under the date of 7 January 1778, records:

> The meeting having under their consideration the state and constitution of the Lodge, that those members incline to raise themselves to the Degree of Mark Mason and Mark Master Mason, and that in time past no benefit has accrued to the Lodge.
>
> Therefore resolved that in time coming all members that shall hereafter raise to the Degree of Mark Mason shall pay one merk Scots but not to obtain the Degree of *Mark Mason* before they are passed Fellow Craft. And that those that shall take the Degree of Mark Master Mason shall pay one shilling and sixpence sterling into the Treasurer for behoof of the Lodge.
>
> None to attain to the Degree of *Mark Master Mason* until they are raised Master.

The first portion of this minute proves that Mark Masonry had been worked, as two degrees, prior to 1778, although no mention of it is made in any previous entry.

These two records must suffice to show that in point of date Mark Masonry worked as a degree or degrees was well established from about the middle of the eighteenth century in Scotland.

Mark Masonry in England

In England, preceding the middle of the eighteenth century, we have nothing in reference to Marks in the Old Charges, or to the Mark Degree in the minutes of lodges either in operative or speculative freemasonry.

When the Mark Degree began to be worked in England is not known. We do know that previous to the union of the two

Grand Lodges the degree was worked under the authority of the Grand Lodge of all England at York, as well as under warrants emanating from Scotland and from the Grand Chapter of Ireland. No separate warrants to hold Mark lodges were issued by the latter, but Royal Arch Chapters were by virtue of their Royal Arch warrants empowered to work the Mark Degree.

There were, however, separate certificates, if desired, for the Mark Degree, which might be conferred on a master mason at any time after he had obtained that degree, whereas he could not obtain the Royal Arch Degree until he had been a Master Mason at least six months.

Pride of place in Mark history in England is generally given to the great Thomas Dunckerley, who held a record number of Provincial Grand Masterships. Hampshire was the first Province placed under his care, and his Patent or Warrant of Appointment was dated 28 February 1767. It is considered probable that about this time Dunckerley had been admitted into the Mark Degree during a visit to the North of England, but exactly when or where is not certain. We know that in a letter to Sir Benjamin Craven, dated 14 January 1792, Dunckerley wrote. 'I was exalted [in the Royal Arch] at Portsmouth in the year 1754.' (See Sadler's *Thomas Dunckerley*, p 248.)

It is almost certain that his own Province was the first in the South of England to have the benefit of his acquired knowledge of the Mark Degree in the form that he had himself received it and we find in fact that the earliest record yet traced of the Mark Degree was at Portsmouth.

Earliest known Mark Minute: Chapter of Friendship, 1769

Before quoting this most important minute and Dunckerley's association therewith, I would observe that 'Moderns' Grand Chapter issued its first Warrants in 1769, in which year seven Chapters were constituted. Amongst these seven was the Chapter of Friendship, Portsmouth, whose Warrant was dated 11 August 1769.

This does not mean that the Royal Arch had not been worked in Portsmouth prior to that time for, as I have shown, Dunckerley himself had been Exalted at Portsmouth in 1754, probably in a Chapter working in connection with the Lodge at the Three Tuns, No 31, in which he had been initiated. What is worthy of note is that the Chapter of Friendship received its Warrant in August 1769 and twenty-one days later we have the first entry in the minutes recording the reference to the two Mark Degrees of Mark Man and Mark Master. The actual entry under date 1 September 1769 was written in Cipher and is reproduced in Alexander Howell's *History of the Phoenix Lodge, No. 257, Chapter of Friendship, No. 257, and Royal Naval Preceptory of Knights Templar, No. 2.*

The translation reads:

> At a Royal Arch Chapter held at the George Tavern in Portsmouth on First Septr. Seventeen hundred and Sixty-nine – Present: Thomas Dunckerley, Esq., William Cook 'Z', Samual Palmer 'H', Thomas Scanville 'J', Henty Dean Philip Joyes and Thomas Webb – The Pro. G.M. Thomas Dunckerley bro't the Warrant of the Chapter and having lately ret'd the 'Mark' he made the bre'n 'Mark Masons' and each chuse their 'Mark' viz. W. Cook, Z^x, S. Palmer, H^x, T. Scanville, J^x, H. Dean,^{x} Philip Joyes,^{x} T. Webb,^{x}. He also told us of this mann'r of Writing which is to be used in the degree w'ch we may give to others so they be FC for Mark Masons and Master M for Mark Masters.

It will be seen that this minute establishes that the Mark Degree, as worked by Dunckerley, was in two sections: Mark Mason for Fellow Craft, and Mark Master for Master Mason.

'This mann'r of writing which is to be used in the degree' alluded to in the minute was, of course, a form of the Mark Cypher. It once constituted an essential part of the traditional explanation of the Degree and carried important secrets with it.

The compiler says in regard to the minutes contained in the Minute Book. 'Many brethren sign their name and add a Mark, although no mention of their receiving the Mark Degree is made in the Volume, and I venture to submit that no Brother received the Royal Arch in this Chapter down to at least 1844, without also receiving the Mark.'

There is another minute which is noteworthy – that a brother could take the Mark alone and need not necessarily take the Royal Arch with it.

> October 21st, 1778. Comp. Palmer, Z, read a letter from Comp. Dunckerley, that we might make Knights Templars if we wanted, and it was resolved to. Brother John Dance took the Mark and chose his Mark. Bro. Dance declined the Arch.

Marquis of Granby Lodge, No 124, Durham (dating back to 1738, although not Constituted until 1763) was working a *Mark Degree in 1773*. The Minutes of 21 December state that, 'Bro Barwick was also made a Mark'd Mason and Bro James Mackinlay raised to the degree of a Master Mason and also made a Mark Mason and paid accordingly.'

St Thomas Lodge (London), No 142, Constituted 1775, was two years later working the *Mark Degree*. 9 August 1777 – 'The Worshipful Master, with the following brethren of this Lodge, were made Mark Masons and Mark Masters' – Fanciful marks are entered against the names of the ten members.

Again on 14 August 1777 – 'Regular Lodge Night' – [the names of fifteen more who were made] 'Mark Masons and also Mark Master Masons' with a note:

> Mark Mason (or 'Mark Man') being for Fellow Craft and the 'Mark Master' for Master Masons.

This indicates that there were apparently two separate degrees worked.

It is not necessary to record later entries in Minutes of lodges for it is evident that Mark Masonry between the 1780s and the Union must have made great progress.

The Bon Accord Mark Lodge, T.I., London

In the year 1851 six brethren, who had taken the Mark Degree in the Bon Accord Chapter in Aberdeen, applied to that Chapter for a commission to make certain brothers in London 'Mark Masters'; this no doubt, because it was thought that the Mark Degree could be given by one brother to another, and need not necessarily be given in lodge at all. The

Bon Accord Chapter replied that they could not grant a 'commission', but if a proper petition was presented they would grant a Charter to the brethren to work the degree in London. The petition was duly sent, and a Charter granted dated 17 September 1851. This is the first record at present known of the chartering of a lodge in England for the sole object of working the Mark, and it is no doubt owing to this that the Bon Accord was allocated the honourable position it holds on the roll of lodges of the Grand Lodge of Mark Master Masons.

The granting of this Charter by a Subordinate Chapter was, however, declared illegal, for it was granted without consulting the Supreme Grand Chapter of Scotland and that authority suspended the Aberdeen Bon Accord Chapter and its Office-bearers.

The pronouncement of the Supreme Grand Royal Arch Chapter of Scotland in 1855, which was issued through the Grand Scribe, was to the effect:

> that the Aberdeen Bon Accord Chapter . . . cannot grant Warrants to any other body of Masons to confer the said Degrees, or dispute its own power in any way whatsoever. That the Chapter of Bon Accord of Aberdeen has thus assumed to itself the powers which can be exercised by the Supreme Chapter alone and are not confirmed on any daughter Chapter, either by its Charter or by the laws of the Supreme Chapter. The Supreme Chapter therefore directs that intimation be made to Companion Rettie to withdraw the Warrant immediately, and to Report at the next Quarterly Communication that the same has been done in order to avoid the necessity of ulterior measures.

This communication was dated 20 June 1855, and on the following 19 September this further communication was issued.

> It having been reported to the Supreme Grand Chapter that no communication had been received from Companion Rettie, First Principal of the Bon Accord Chapter, Aberdeen, in answer to their former communication called upon the Chapter to report that they had withdrawn the Mark Warrant which had been improperly and illegally issued by them for constituting a Mark Masters' Lodge in

London, are unanimously of opinion that such conduct infers a want of respect towards this Supreme Body and a refusal to comply with its decisions. They therefore . . . suspend the said Chapter of Bon Accord, Aberdeen, from their privileges as a body of Royal Arch Masons aye and until such time as effect shall have been given to the order made upon them and the Warrant in question delivered up in order to its being cancelled.

The Aberdeen Bon Accord Chapter, claiming to be in the right, decided to return their own Charter to the Grand Chapter. They also passed the following resolution: 'Being aware that the Arch and other subordinate Degrees connected therewith were wrought by the Knights Templar Encampment in Aberdeen many years previous to the formation of the Supreme Chapter, and that the Knights Templar Encampment never gave up their inherent right of working these Degrees, therefore resolve to apply to the St George Aboyne Knights Templar Encampment for a Warrant or Charter to work the Royal Arch Degree and other subordinate Degrees connected therewith, and that the Office-bearers be appointed to carry this resolution into effect.'

The Grand Lodge of Mark Master Masons of England, 1856

As I shall later be quoting verbatim from the historical introduction which appeared in the early editions of the MMM Constitutions by Order of the Most Worshipful Grand Master it will avoid unnecessary duplication of the particulars connected with the formation of the Grand Lodge of Mark Master Masons in England.

The First Edition of the Constitutions, 1856/7

The first meeting of the New Grand Lodge was held in June 1856, and on 30 May 1857, a further meeting was convened. Shortly afterwards was published:

> Constitution / of the / Grand Lodge of Mark Masters / of / England and Wales, / and the Colonies and Possessions of the / British Crown: / Being the / Regulations / for the / Government of the Craft: / Published under the superintendence of the General

Board / and by the authority of the Grand Lodge / London: / Printed by J. Donnison, Liverpool Street, / Bishopsgate / [rule] / 1857.

It consisted of thirty-six pages, including title page and a contents leaf. The binding was in red cloth with blind stamped borders on sides, lettered on the upper cover in gilt:

GRAND LODGE / OF / MARK MASTERS / [rule] / CONSTITUTION, 1856.
Copies of this first edition are said to be very rare.

Another edition, also in the red cloth binding, was published, still retaining on its cover the date of 1856 but its title page is dated 1864.

This edition had some alterations to its title page. In place of the words 'Colonies and Possessions' it has 'Colonies and Dependencies'; again, in place of 'For the Government of the Craft' it has 'For the Government of the Members of the Degree of Mark Master'; the printer had been changed and the imprint reads: 'Printed by R. S. Warrington, 2 New King Street, St Martin's Lane, W.C. 1864'.

Brethren will notice that these two editions 1857 and 1864 were in red cloth binding reminiscent of the colour for Royal Arch Constitutions. Later editions are all in blue cloth bindings. With the edition of 1864 and those editions down to 1879 there was prefixed a preliminary historical introduction. The wording is somewhat abbreviated in the 1879 edition so as to allow for the inclusion of later events. I therefore quote the text as it first appeared in the edition of 1864:

Origin of the Grand Lodge of Mark Masters of England, &c., as set forth in a Memorandum for the information of the Supreme Grand Royal Arch Chapter of Scotland, with reference to the Status and Position of the Degree of Mark Master in England and Wales, especially in connection with its working under the jurisdiction of The Grand Lodge of Mark Masters of England and Wales, and the Colonies and Possessions of the British Crown.

Previous to the Union of the Two Grand Lodges in England, respectively held at York and London, effected in 1813, under the Title of The United Grand Lodge of England, the Mark

Degree was regularly worked under the authority of The Grand Lodge, meeting from time immemorial at York. At the said Union, in 1813, the Mark Degree was abolished as a separate degree, such portion as was deemed of importance being, as stated, retained, but incorporated partly in the degree of Master Mason, and partly in the ceremony described as the completion of that degree, and known as The Holy Royal Arch. One of the Articles of the Declaration agreed to at such Union being: 'Pure and Ancient Masonry consists of three degrees, and no more, including the Holy Royal Arch.'

Notwithstanding this declaration, the Mark Degree continued to be extensively worked in the Northern and Midland districts of England, in some cases the lodges being held under their immemorial constitution, derived from the Old Athol York Grand Lodge; in some cases in connection with, or under the authority of, Knights Templar Encampments; and in some places the degree continued to be conferred (and this until very recently in a lodge of Fellow-Crafts; the lodge or lodges so conferring the degree being under the jurisdiction of The United Grand Lodge of England; the fact of the degree being thus conferred being, probably, unknown to the latter body. The same circumstances, though to a limited extent, have been found to exist in the South of England.

One or other of the Supreme bodies exercising masonic jurisdiction in Scotland, Ireland, and America, has always regarded the Mark Degree as an essential and integral portion of ancient freemasonry.

In England, as has been shown, the knowledge and working of the degree has never been lost, though it has been more or less in abeyance, its estimation varying according to varying circumstances.

In the Colonies much difficulty has been encountered from the establishment of lodges under different jurisdictions, some recognising the Mark Degree and some altogether ignoring it.

To remedy this state of things, and to restore the degree to its rightful position in connection with the masonic system, an attempt was made, about the year 1855, to obtain its recognition by the United Grand Lodge of England, and a committee consisting of members of that Grand Lodge and of members of the Supreme Grand Royal Arch Chapter of England was appointed to investigate and report upon the subject of the Mark Degree.

Some members of this committee were already Mark Masters; those who had not taken the Degree had it conferred upon them in the Albany Lodge (time immemorial), Isle of Wight, and in other old lodges, and some in the Bon Accord Mark Lodge, then recently established in London, under a charter received from the Bon Accord Royal Arch Chapter of Aberdeen.

The report of the committee approved by the MW Grand Master pronouncing the Mark Degree as in their opinion not positively essential, but a graceful appendage to the degree of Fellow-Craft, was presented to the United Grand Lodge of England at the Quarterly Communication in March 1856, and was unanimously adopted.

At the next ensuing Quarterly Communication of The United Grand Lodge of England, on special motion, duly proposed and seconded, that portion of the minutes of the previous Quarterly Communication referring to the Mark Degree was non-confirmed, and the status in quo ante was resumed.

The legality of the origin of the Bon Accord lodge having been called in question by the Supreme Grand Chapter of Scotland, many brethren anxious to take the degree, owing to prominence being given to it by the recent discussions, declined to receive it until authorised regulations for its government should be established. Several earnest masons, anxious for the propagation of the degree without waiting to see what steps would be taken by the members of the Bon Accord Lodge to remedy the defect of its original constitution (should such be proved to exist), applied for and received Charters from the Supreme Grand Chapter of Scotland, under the authority of which they opened lodges and conferred the Degree of Mark Master in London, and other parts of England.

The members of the Bon Accord Lodge, together with

several other Mark Master Masons who had taken the degree in various old (time immemorial) lodges, gladly welcoming the increasing appreciation of the Mark Degree, but not approving what they could not but regard as a systematic attempt to introduce a foreign supreme masonic authority into England, resolved to constitute a Grand Lodge with jurisdiction over the Mark Degree in this country and its possessions, which at once received the adhesion of many of the old (time immemorial) lodges; amongst them

    The Northumberland and Berwick   Newcastle upon Tyne
    The Royal Cumberland   Bath
    The Old Kent   London

and the countenance and approval of the representatives of other lodges who did not at once yield their allegiance, viz.:

    The Albany   Isle of Wight
    The Howe   Birmingham, &c.

    The Right Honourable Lord Leigh (Craft) Provincial Grand Master of Warwickshire, a thoroughly constitutional mason, and a personal friend of the MW Grand Master of England, was unanimously elected Grand Master of the new organisation, and lent most valuable assistance in framing its laws and maturing its system of government. Other adhesions of old lodges, with applications for new charters were received, and letters of approval and encouragement were addressed to the executive from many of the most influential masons throughout the country.

    The first meeting of The New Grand Lodge was held in June, 1856, when a desire for a general union of all the Mark Masters in England under one head was most warmly expressed. To give effect to this desire, a meeting was convened; Lord Leigh addressing a circular to the representatives of the various Mark Lodges, wherever they could be found; and at this meeting the course recently adopted in the formation of the Mark Grand Lodge was formally approved; additional adhesions were given in, and a Committee appointed to concert measures for rendering the Union as effective as possible.

    Meanwhile, the representatives of the lodges holding Charters from the Supreme Grand Chapter of Scotland became desirous of a General Union under one Supreme Body in this country; and a meeting of the brethren holding office in those lodges was held, at which resolutions approving a Union with this Grand Lodge were unanimously adopted.

Copies of the circular alluded to above addressed by Lord Leigh to the various lodges of Mark Masters, and of the proceedings of the representatives of lodges under Scotch Charters, are enclosed for information.

From the date of this last meeting to the present time, this Grand Lodge has gone on increasing in numbers, position, and influence, and we have very nearly 2,000 registered members, to which additions are being made at the rate of about 400 per annum.

Of old (time immemorial) lodges now acknowledging the supremacy of this Grand Lodge there are:

The Northumberland and Berwick	Newcastle upon Tyne
The Royal Cumberland	Bath
The Kent	London
The Prince Edward	Halifax, Yorkshire
The Friendship	Devonport
The Minerva	Hull
The Benevolent	Stockport
The Portsmouth	Portsmouth

Of the lodges originally holding Charters from Scotland there are:

The Bon Accord	London
The Thistle	London
The Cheltenham and Keystone	Cheltenham
The West Lancashire	Liverpool

Several other existing lodges are in negotiation with us for terms of union, and we have granted 49 original Charters for lodges in England and the Colonies.

In June, 1860, Lord Leigh was succeeded as Grand Master by the Earl of Carnarvon, and in June, 1863, the latter nobleman was succeeded by Viscount Holmesdale, MP.

> The Executive of The Grand Lodge of Mark Masters of England and Wales, and the Colonies and Dependencies of the British

Crown, rely with confidence upon the statement here submitted, as proving it to be *de facto* and *de jure* the Supreme Governing Body of the Mark Degree in this part of the United Kingdom and its Colonies and Possessions, with as legitimate and indefeasible a claim to all the rights, privileges, and prerogatives, appertaining to such a Body as can be claimed by any other existing Supreme Masonic Jurisdiction. It does not seek aggrandisement by territorial aggression and is prepared to maintain its right against those who invade its rule. It is ready and desirous of uniting in friendly correspondence, and in amicable relationship with other Bodies exercising similar jurisdiction in their respective countries, and to lend a willing aid in promoting the best interests of the Degree of Mark Master, and of Freemasonry generally. As a means to this end, and with a view to promote that Masonic unity and harmony so desirable, it calls upon the Supreme Grand Chapter of Scotland to abstain from further issue of Mark Charters in this country, and urges a recall of those already issued, in accordance with the terms and stipulations therein contained. It asks, and is ready to concede, a mutual recognition and a friendly representation by duly appointed Brethren from one Supreme Body to the other.

By Order of Viscount Holmesdale, M.P., Most Worshipful Grand Master.

[*Signed*] FREDERICK BINCKES,
Grand Secretary.

LONDON, *8th September 1864.*

The Mark Degree in Ireland

A writer on *Some Notes on Irish Masonry* who signed himself 'Gimel', says:

Those who have been accustomed to find the Royal Arch in close connection with the Craft, and the Mark degree optional, are surprised to find the Mark obligatory before receiving the R.A. In Ireland, the Mark is an honorary advancement preliminary to the Arch, and no business can be transacted at a Mark meeting except the Installation, or the advancement of candidates. All ordinary business is carried out in the Chapter. Here I may say that I consider the English Mark a finer degree. Our Mark Ceremony does not contain the 'Mark Man' part, and although one must be installed Very Worshipful Master (Installed Master of a Mark Lodge) before presiding in the R.A., one's election as Excellent

King of a Chapter entitles one to the Mark Chair, and no separate certificate is issued. The Mark Chair is merely certified by a stamp on the back of the King's Certificate.

Further, before being installed, a Brother must have completed his term as Master of a Craft Lodge, and have served as either High Priest or Scribe.

Our R.A. exhibits such striking differences that English Companions feel quite at sea. This is partly owing to our degree commemorating an event about five hundred years earlier than that which the English R.A. is based on. The combination of the old degrees of Excellent and Super-Excellent Mason with our R.A. bring it more into line with Scotland than England. The time limit before taking the R.A. is six months.

Both Mark and Arch can be given on the same day.

Freemasonry in Ireland prior to Grand Lodge

Brothers Lepper and Crossle in their *History of the Grand Lodge of Ireland* put forward the conclusions they are disposed to draw from the evidences of freemasonry in Ireland prior to 1717, stating 'that the main points that seem to them essentially demonstrated are these: that at least as early as 1688, Lodges of operative Freemasons were admitting speculative members 'in the new way', as the 'Commencements harangue' [of 1688 at Trinity College] says; . . . and that these speculative freemasons thus admitted [not all in the Trinity College, of course] carried the Craft into the most remote corners of Ireland within a very few years. Indeed, the rapidity with which the Craft extended was so amazing [as is shown by the distribution of the first Warrants] that in order to account for its presence in 1732 in districts far removed from the Capital one is tempted to assign a very much earlier date than 1688 for the admission of speculative freemasons in Ireland'.

There is ample proof in the enactments of the Grand Lodge of Ireland itself that there were a considerable number of Independent lodges working under Time Immemorial usage in or about 1730. In one interesting instance the antiquity of the lodge applying for a Warrant is acknowledged in the Warrant itself, where the word 'Erect' has been altered to read 'Continue a Lodge of Free Masons', etc. Evidence points to

Irish masonry having had in its custody a very full esoteric tradition.

We know that there is evidence of the Royal Arch Degree in Ireland at least as early as 1744 and that Mark Masonry was certainly known in Ireland some years later, probably in the 1770's.

The Earliest known Irish Record – Kinsdale, 1775

This, the earliest known record of the conferring of a Mark Degree in Ireland, is contained in a certificate of 27 August 1775, granted by the Knights Templars of Kinsdale, County Cork. In this certificate the recipient, James Dennison, is styled a Mark Mason. A photograph of this certificate is given in Brother Grantham's book *An Introduction to Mark Masonry.*

The Present Form of MMM Degree in Ireland

Brother Philip Crossle, in his interesting *History of the T.I. Irish Lodge*, known as Lodge Two, says that it was responsible for the introduction into Ireland of the present form of the Mark Master Mason Degree. John Fowler, for many years secretary of that lodge, in the year 1825, when he received the papers relating to the 33rd Degree of the A and ASR from Charleston, in America, also received a Mark Master Mason Ritual from the same place. This ritual apparently differed very considerably from what Irish Masons theretofore knew as the Arch Degree (of the Royal Arch Group), or the Mark Master's Degree (or Cain's Mark of the Red Cross Mason's group), and it had no status in the A and ASR. Struck by the beauty of this American Ritual, John Fowler, in his capacity of a Sovereign Grand Inspector of Ireland, on 13 December 1825, constituted a Meeting of the members of Lodge Two into 'a lawful lodge of Mark Master Masons'. . . . The degree was not recognised officially till some time in the 1840's, when Grand Lodge took cognisance of it by registering Mark Master Masons on the Grand Lodge Register. Subsequently the Degree was transferred to the Grand Royal Arch Chapter of Ireland.

Symbolism of the Mark Degree

Whilst the symbolism is very fully shown in the progress of the degree itself, and will, of course, commend itself to the intelligent masonic student, I think that a few words may be quoted from Mackey's *Book of the Chapter*, as these supplement to some extent those given in the Lectures on the Tracing Board in the English rituals.

> The symbolic allusion of the Indenting Chisel and the Mallet is one of the first things to which the attention of the Candidate is directed. The Chisel and Mallet are used by Operative Masons to hew, cut, carve and indent their work; but as Mark Masters, we are taught to employ them for a more noble and glorious purpose; they teach us to hew, cut, carve and indent the principles of morality and virtue on our minds.
>
> *The Chisel* morally demonstrates the advantages of discipline and education. The mind, like the diamond in its original state, is rude and unpolished; but as the effect of the chisel on the external coat soon presents to view the latent beauties of the diamond, so education discovers the latent virtues of the mind, and draws them forth to range the large field of matter and space to display the summit of human knowledge, our duty to God and Man.
>
> *The Mallet* morally teaches us to correct irregularities, and to reduce man to a proper level; so that, by quiet deportment, he may, in the school of discipline, learn to be content.
>
> What the Mallet is to the workman, enlightened reason is to the passions; it curbs ambition, it depresses envy, it moderates anger, and it encourages good dispositions; whence arises among good masons that comely order,
>
> 'While nothing earthly gives, or can destroy,
> The Soul's calm sunshine, and the heartfelt joy.'

The Keystone, in this degree, is evidently an allusion to the Tessera Hospitales, or hospitable tokens, amongst the ancients and which are thus described by Dr Adam Clarke.

> A small oblong square piece of wood, bone, stone, or ivory, was taken, and divided into two equal parts, on which each of the parties wrote his own name, and then interchanged it with the other. This was carefully preserved, and handed down, even to posterity, in the same family; and by producing this when they

travelled, it gave a mutual claim to the bearers of kind reception and hospitable entertainment at each other's houses.

In the passage from the second chapter of Revelations, which is read during the presentation of the Keystone, it is most probable that by the White stone and the 'new name', St John referred to these tokens of alliance and friendship. With these views, the symbolic allusion of the Keystone in the Mark Degree is very apparent. It is intended to denote the firm and friendly alliance which exists between Mark Masters, and to indicate that by the possession of this token, and the new name inscribed upon it, and which is known only to those who have received it in the progress of the initiation, a covenant has been instituted that, in all future time, and under every circumstance of danger or distress, will secure the kind and friendly assistance of those who are the possessors of the same token.

The Mark Master is thus, by the reception of this mystic sign, adopted into the fraternity of all other Mark Masons, and entitled to all the rights and privileges which belong exclusively to the partakers in the meaning of the same significant stone. The Keystone of a Mark Master is, therefore, the symbol of a fraternal covenant among those who are engaged in the common search after Divine Truth.

Earlier English MMM Ritual

In the earlier rituals published by Lewis we find in the Introductory General History these very apt words:

> The speculative value of Mark Masonry consists in its inculcating order, regularity, and discipline. Precision and punctuality should mark the execution of every office, station, and ceremony, and the unexpected importance of the leading symbol of the Degree should teach the true Freemason not to overlook or undervalue the smallest item of knowledge submitted for his consideration – for in this consists the true strength of the Fraternity. As that which was rejected of the builders has become the headstone of the corner, so in Mark Masonry the curiously formed wrought Key Stone in its turn becomes the strengthening culmination of the Arch, binding the whole structure together by a peculiar property contained in mathematical form.

While the Perfect Ashlar or Wrought stone shows itself to be naturally the most fitting form for perpendicular walls reared to any desired height, in the same way the principle of the wedge underlying that of the keystone of every arch shows how strength and union may be secured with the advantage of a covered way. The wedge has been also used as an implement for the cleavage of stubborn and obstinate matter, and thus illustrates in a tangible form the justice of The Supreme Overseer of the Universe, while the Marked Stone used in Mark Masonry symbolises the all-sustaining strength of the Creator. The principle of the arch, it has been found by architects, is far more ancient that it was at one time supposed, nor was it confined to comparatively recent races of mankind, or races immediately under the known influence of ordinary progressive civilisation.

The amazing discoveries of the last fifty or sixty years have materially extended the sphere of our technical acquaintance with ancient forms of edification, and show that the simplest forms have ever been adopted for purposes of use and beauty; that mind becomes lost in the contemplation of the resources of that Divine Mind, the soul of the Infinite Universe, from which these ideas primarily emanated.

What, then, should the devout Freemason do, but humbly honour and devoutly adore the Source of all Light and Truth, 'in whom we live, and move, and have our being'.

The Stone: its Inspection and Rejection

The Stones of the Temple, we are told, were cubical – the symbol of perfection. The original Tabernacle and afterwards the Sanctum Sanctorum were cubical in shape, and all the stones employed in their building partook of the cubical form, hence illustrating truth, perfection, and completeness.

At the building of the Temple each Craftsman was to finish his work according to the instructions given to him, namely, a perfect square or cubical.

The Overseers were to receive no other work; hence if a stone was neither square nor oblong when it was presented, it had to be rejected.

The three inspections would appear to be unnecessary, yet they allegorically teach important considerations. The first inspection represents the 'worldly wise'; the second, 'religious formalism', and the third, 'the spiritual tests'.

Let us consider this symbolical or allegorical lesson from which we learn these truths.

(1) The 'world wise' accept a man's work as it appears when presented; he may have earnestly devoted himself to the business of this life and have accumulated a large fortune; he may have been an active and honoured Statesman, or the world may be aware of the multiplicity of his writings. The inspection of the world may, although not according to true law, pronounce it as beautiful in workmanship and let it pass.

(2) The inspection of 'formalism' sees the beauty and singularity, and permits this specimen of religious philosophy to pass because of its seeming beautiful workmanship.

(3) The presenting for final approval – the Spiritual Test. The Master views it from a different standpoint and sees that the 'life work' has not been wrought for the good of others, but for the own individual selfish gratification of its worker, and consequently devoid of that beauty which alone renders it fit for a place in the Temple, and is therefore quite useless.

There is in the Mark Degree symbolism a much greater significance than that which can be seen at first glance.

The Hour Glass. In the Lecture on the Tracing Board we are told that 'This emblem reminds us, by the quick passage of its sands, of the transitory nature of human life'. It reminds us that 'Time Flies'. In the MMs' degree we were reminded of the emblem of mortality – the skull, 'Remember Death', or as portrayed in the Dance of Death with the words 'Memento Mori'. Brethren may have seen some of the Old Craft rituals which were printed within the Dance of Death pictorial borders. This was not intended purely as a pictorial ornamentation, but conveyed the meaning of that which is veiled in allegory and illustrated by symbols.

In the days when the Mark was conferred on the Fellow Craft, the symbol of the Hour Glass was a warning to the initiate to make the most of his time for this earthly life will one day come to an end. When he received the MMs' degree he figuratively represented the Master Hiram Abiff who had come to an untimely death rather than betray the trust reposed in him. But he also learned that there was the resurrection, the raising to an eternal life in the Grand Lodge above. In the MMM degree he had placed before him the wisdom of conforming in all things to the will of the Grand Overseer of the Universe when eventually in the RA he would discover that which was lost to those who had not heeded the warning of fidelity.

Masons' Marks

In a chapter on Mark Masonry, Laurie, the Scottish masonic historian gives a good deal of space to the Marks of the workmen, including the use of the Mark, and a large number of illustrations, ranging in date from 1128 to that of Robert Burns, inscribed upon the Bible presented by him to 'Highland Mary' [see illustration]. He also speaks of the manner of giving instruction in reading the Marks, and gives the following interesting dialogue:

THE MASON'S MARK OF ROBERT BURNS
(Illustration taken from Hunter's 'Burns as a Mason)

Q. How many points has your Mark got?
A. Three Points.
Q. To what do they allude?
A. To the three points of an equilateral triangle.
Q. Please demonstrate it as an operative Mason.
A. A point has position, without length, breadth, or thickness; a line has length, without breadth or thickness, and terminates in two points; and three lines of equal length,

> placed at equal angles to each other, form an equilateral triangle, —— which is the primary figure in geometry.
> Q. Please to explain this figure as a Speculative Mason.
> A. The equilateral triangle represents the Trinity in Unity, —— The Great Architect of the Universe, having no material form, exists, pervading all space; the Creator of all things, Governor of all animate and inanimate nature, Fountain of Wisdom; whose greatness, perfection, and Glory is incomprehensible, and whose loving-kindness and tender mercies are over all His other works.

In classing the workmen, due regard is had for the manner in which they were ranked at the building of King Solomon's Temple. These are made familiar in America in the Master's degree.

The Mark Master is regarded as an Overseer, and is thus referred to: 'The duty of the Foreman, or, as he is occasionally designated, the Mark Overseer, was to direct and instruct the Fellow Crafts or Markmen in the details of the work upon which they were engaged, and see that it was completed, according to the plan furnished.'

In regard to the ritual used in Scotland, Instructions for each degree are provided, and those for the Mark may be inferred from the following explanation by Laurie.

> The Form of Initiation and legend of the Mark Overseer is of Eastern character, referring to the preparation of the materials for building Solomon's Temple at Jerusalem, and navigating the rafts on which they were conveyed along the coast of the great [*ie* Mediterranean] Sea, guided by a lighthouse situated on one of the peaks of Mount Lebanon. The Speculative Lecture inculcates a constant practice of the principles of morality, in every position in life, beautifully illustrated by the operations of the Mason, under the guidance of scientific rules fashioning with persevering industry the rude block into the perfect form, having it approved and marked for its place in the intended building; and applying the illustration both to the upbuilding of the individual mind as well as to the moral fabric of society, and pointing to the hope that all may become living stones of God's own temple. Such a system of scientific and moral discipline was evidently well adapted to the

circumstances of the craftsmen, whose associations required him frequently to wander to great distances, in search of employment, and while residing among strangers, enabled him to teach by his example, and to live in concord and good fellowship among the members with whom his labours were associated.

These few notes which I have attempted do not profess to have done more than touch upon the fringe of the study of the Mark Degree, but I trust that they will have conveyed some information which will prove of interest and encourage others to seek more light on this time-honoured degree.

8

FREEMASONRY IN SCOTLAND IN 1717

George Draffen

WHAT WAS THE position of freemasonry in Scotland when, in 1717, the Grand Lodge of England was founded in the City of Westminster, London? It is almost certain that the membership of the 'four old Lodges' which met at the Goose and Gridiron tavern to found the first Grand Lodge in the world was made up of gentlemen and artisans. It is unlikely that there was in any of the four lodges an operative mason, *ie* a man who earned his daily bread as a stone-mason. The position in Scotland at that time was very different.

In 1717 there were in existence at least twenty lodges in widely separated parts of the country. There were lodges in Edinburgh, in Kilwinning, in Inverness, in Dundee, in Stirling, in Perth, in Aberdeen, in Glasgow, and in other smaller towns throughout Scotland. It must not be assumed, however, that these lodges were the Scottish counterparts of the four old London lodges. Far from it, for the majority of these active Scottish lodges were still composed of operative members, that is to say men who earned their living at the building trade. On the other hand most of the lodges had a smaller or greater number of non-operatives, that is to say members who had no connection with the trade of a stone-mason and who had joined the lodge out of curiosity or as honorary members, or maybe as patrons. In 1717, freemasonry as we know it today was still, in Scotland, in the transitional stage. And yet there are curious discrepancies to be found.

The Lodge of Edinburgh (Mary's Chapel) had admitted non-operatives to its membership as early as 1634 and the Lodge of Aberdeen had admitted some twelve members of the University by 1670. In neither of these lodges did the non-operatives take control until well after 1717. In the Lodge at Haughfoot, which worked from 1702 until 1764 (and never took a Charter from the Grand Lodge of Scotland), *all* the members were non-operatives. One might have expected such a lodge to be found in one of the larger centres of population – but Haughfoot is a small village in the more inaccessible hinterland of the borders between Scotland and England. That a small village in a then somewhat remote part of Scotland should have a fully-functioning *speculative* lodge is one of the mysteries of early Scottish freemasonry.

The organisation of the Mason Trade in Scotland was under greater central control by authority than it was in England. The *Schaw Statutes* of 1598 and 1599 mention three lodges, at Edinburgh, at Kilwinning and at Stirling, as being in control, under the overall supervision of the Master Mason to the King of Scotland, of all work in three different parts of the country. From other sources it seems likely that lodges in St Andrews, Dundee and, possibly, Aberdeen, exercised similar control in the north-eastern part of the country.

By 1717 the use of stone as a building material in England had been largely superseded by brick, at least in so far as house-building was concerned. This resulted in a decline in the Mason Trade. That was not the case in Scotland, where stone continued to be used as the main building material. The Mason Trade remained active and provided employment all over the country – and the lodges continued to flourish. This explains in large measure why the Scottish lodges remained active long after the English Operative lodges had begun to decline.

The admission of non-operatives into the Scottish lodges is something that has yet to be explained. In the earliest days it was probably done as something of a gesture to a patron who had given a large amount of work to the lodge. Later it may have been curiosity or possibly an antiquarian desire to become a member of an organisation which was in some danger of dying out and thus perpetuate it. This motive is still present today in many of the old Guilds in the Scottish cities: indeed those Guilds which have survived are now mainly convivial clubs whose members are in no way connected with the Trade of the Guild. It is possible that a similar motive brought the first non-operatives into the Mason Guilds. Whatever the reason, we are still in the dark as to why these non-operatives began to turn, slowly but surely, an operative Craft into a Speculative Society.

By 1717 the process of turning the Operative lodge into a Speculative lodge had, in England, advanced sufficiently far to permit of the founding of the first Grand Lodge – an organisation quite unknown to the Operative lodges. In Scotland the process had not advanced so far and it was not until 1736 that the non-operatives were strong enough to found the Grand Lodge of Scotland.

By 1717 the Scottish operative lodges were, in the main, still composed of actual stone-craftsmen with a sprinkling of non-operatives. The ceremonies used at the admission of both kinds of members were brief – if the evidence of the *Register House MS*, the *Haughfoot Fragment* and the *Kevan MS* are to be taken as indicative of the ceremonies worked. Only two 'degrees' were known, Apprentice and Fellow. In this case it must be understood that the title 'Fellow' was equivalent to Master and a Fellow was entitled to employ apprentices. He was in fact the master of his trade. Even today the word Fellow is still used in this sense in connection with many professional bodies, such as the Royal College of Surgeons, where to be a Fellow is an indication that one has reached the highest rank in the profession. The Third Degree, as we know it today was quite unknown in Scotland and the earliest record of it is in the year 1728. It was unknown in at least one lodge as late as 1750, although the lodge had been working since 1701.

The Scottish lodges in 1717 still exercised a considerable control over entry into the building trade in each City or Burgh. It was, in some respects, the equivalent of the modern trade union. It collected dues, looked after the widows and orphans of its members and, through the Dean of Guild, exercised control over the type of buildings erected within the Burgh boundaries. Apart from the Lodge at Haughfoot, the Scottish lodges, in 1717, did not allow their non-operative members to have any say in the running of the lodge. It was not, for example, until 1728 that the Lodge of Edinburgh elected a non-operative to the office of Warden.

In contrast to England the Scottish lodges in 1717 did not meet in taverns. They met in premises belonging to the lodge and at least one of these old lodge buildings still survives and is in use today as a lodge room. This lodge room, known as St John's Chapel, belongs to Canongate Kilwinning, No 2, and was consecrated in the first half of the eighteenth century. This is the oldest lodge room in the world, and a visitor to the lodge room today feels that he is in a hallowed place, a place which has remained unchanged for close on two hundred and fifty years. Many of the other old seventeenth-century lodge rooms have been pulled down in the name of progress and the lodge room of the Lodge of Edinburgh (Mary's Chapel) was demolished in 1787, having been built in 1504.

The Scottish lodges do not appear to have had documents corresponding to the Old Charges which were held in such high esteem in England. On the other hand copies of the *Schaw Statutes* and the St Clair Charters are to be found along with copies of the English Old Charges, the latter obviously having been brought to Scotland by travelling brethren.

The student who would delve deeper into the early history of the Craft in Scotland should read Murray Lyon's *History of the Lodge of Edinburgh (Mary's Chapel)*, R. S. Lindsay's *History of Lodge Holyrood House (St Luke)* and Harry Carr's *History of Lodge Mother Kilwinning*. These three volumes will provide a complete study of the Scottish Craft from its earliest operative days to the beginning of the present century.

9

RUDYARD KIPLING – FREEMASON

Raymond Karter

FREEMASONRY, TO THE earnest and reflective mind, opens up vast fields of study which will yield much profit and pleasure. Therefore, it is not surprising that many men of the highest order of intellect, men of thought and action in many lands, have been drawn to its fellowship. The portals of freemasonry have welcomed soldiers such as Wellington, Washington, Garibaldi, Mazzini; the philosophers Adam Smith, Locke and Dugald Stewart; and such writers as Burns, Scott, Goethe, Voltaire, Lessing and Tolstoy. Here and there in general literature, the brotherhood of writers reveals traces of masonic influence, but the young mason in search of reading which will give him greater insight into the spirit of masonry should select the works of Kipling. Eminently readable, these provide a fruitful source of good and lively literature with an important inner core. I am ever grateful to the knowledgeable friend whose advice led me to enjoyment of this author, and by this inadequate appreciation of Kipling I am trying to share my discovery with others who have set out to discover 'the trodden ways of wisdom and the quiet paths of peace', for no other author openly uses so many direct masonic phrases, so many meaningful allusions, in so many stories and poems.

Kipling was born in Bombay on 30 December 1865. He was sent as a boy to England where he was educated at the United Services College in Devon. In *Stalky & Co* he affords a graphic picture of his school days and school mates. On leaving school he returned to India and joined the Indian Civil Service. After a few years he threw off the shackles of officialdom and found his proper sphere in journalism and literature.

Rudyard Kipling was fortunate in his parents. His father, Principal of the School of Art at Lahore, was the author of a book entitled *Beast and Man in India*, and the son inherited to a large degree the father's keen powers of observation and his love of India and its peoples. His mother was a Scotswoman – a MacDonald – and to her the son dedicated his first published book. This was *Plain Tales from the Hills*, dedicated to the 'wittiest lady in India'. To her also he addressed that exquisite poetic tribute to mother love, *Mother o' Mine*. Fortunate in his parents, Kipling may also have been fortunate in his natal city, Bombay, whose cosmopolitan atmosphere stirred his pride in *The Seven Seas*. It was in Lahore, though, that he was born into freemasonry, in Lodge Hope and Perseverance, No 782 EC there. His initiation was by special dispensation, as it took place in 1885, at which time he was only twenty years of age. He refers to this fact in an autobiographical work *Something of Myself*, saying it was 'Because the Lodge hoped for a good Secretary'. He goes on to say rather modestly 'They did not get him but I helped, and got Father to advise in decorating the bare walls of the Masonic Hall with hangings after the prescription of Solomon's Temple'. An interesting point is that the minutes of his raising are entered in his own handwriting, he having acted as Secretary to the meeting where he was raised.

He showed an unusual grasp of the tenets of freemasonry from his earliest days and brought his intellect and intelligence into play so ably that only four months after his raising he read a paper on the 'Origins of the Craft in general and of the First Degree in particular'. Three months later he gave an address on 'Popular Views on Freemasonry'.

He was advanced to the Mark Degree in Mark Lodge Fidelity, No 98 in Lahore in 1887. Later, in England, he was constituted an honorary member of the Motherland Lodge, No 3861, London. He was affiliated as such at the Consecration of this lodge on 28 June 1918. On that particular occasion there was printed a Souvenir Menu on which appeared 'Song of the Native Born' personally selected by Brother Rudyard Kipling, QM, for the occasion.

> A health to the Native-born (Stand up!)
> We're six white men a-row
> All bound to sing of the little things we care about,
> All bound to fight for the little things we care about,
> With the weight of a six-fold blow!
> By the might of our cable-tow (Take hands!)
> From the Orkneys to the Horn,
> All round the world (and a little loop to pull it by)
> All round the world (and a little strap to buckle it)
> A health to the Native-born.

In 1922 he became a Founder Member of the lodge attached to the War Graves Commission, and it was at his suggestion that it was most beautifully named 'The Builders of the Silent Cities'.

Of interest to masons is a letter of Kipling's written in reply to an enquiry regarding his masonic experiences. He says: 'In reply to your letter, I was Secretary for some years of Lodge Hope and Perseverance, No 782, Lahore, which included Brethren of at least four creeds, I was entered by a member of the Brahma Somo (a Hindu): passed by a Mohammedan and raised by an Englishman. Our Tyler was an Indian Jew. We met, of course, on the level, and the only difference anyone would notice was that at some of the banquets, some of the brethren who were debarred by Caste rules from eating foods not ceremonially prepared sat over empty plates. I had the good fortune to be able to arrange a series of informal lectures by Brethren of various faiths on the Baptismal ceremonies of their religions'. (*The Times*, London, 16 January 1925).

In 1929 Kipling presented to his Mother Lodge at Lahore a gavel composed of stone from the quarries, from which was obtained the material for the building of King Solomon's Temple at Jerusalem.

Rudyard Kipling had a direct connection with Scottish freemasonry insomuch that he was constituted an honorary member of Lodge Canongate Kilwinning No 2, on 4 October 1899. He was the elected Poet Laureate of that lodge during the years 1905–1908.

For full appreciation of Kipling, it is advisable to know something of the environment in which he was born and nurtured, and to have at least faint acquaintance with the peoples and ancient civilisation of India. Even cursory study will show that their records, handed down from time immemorial, reveal a standard of ethics and morality different, but in no degree inferior, to those which prevail in the Western Hemisphere. Our interest should be specifically directed to the customs peculiar to the ancient builders. In India there are certain peculiar customs and usages observed by the Architects and Builders – These have been aptly described by Sir Purdon Clarke in a paper on 'The Tracing Board in Eastern Operative Masonry' (Proceedings Quatuor Coronati). The Indian builder was seemingly independent of working plans scored with minute details of elevations and ground sections. Instead of paper, he used sectional lined boards on which to draft his plans, and these Tracing Boards are the key to the Mystery of their Craft. The Egyptians and Persians too, employed this method of enlargement by squaring and the tracing boards were preciously preserved. The Priests were custodians of the Boards, and a special room in the Temple was set apart for the Temple Architect and the plans on his Tracing Board. The mysteries of this Craft have been carefully guarded as an inheritance from generation to generation. It is interesting to observe the kinship between our ornaments and Tracing Boards and these ancient customs and mysteries, but that is too absorbing a story to pursue here if we wish to continue the subject of Kipling.

When one commences the search for direct references and masonic terms in Kipling's works, the treasure is easily found, indeed it is prolific. Of his poems, *The Mother Lodge, The Widow of Windsor, My New Cut Ashlar*, and *The Palace* are all purely masonic in import. In his stories, the allusions and illustrations are also frequent, some of them 'heled and concealed', and others quite direct and obvious. One of the best and finest of his short stories, *The Man Who Would Be King*, has an undeniable masonic significance. Another – *With the Main Guard* – is subtly threaded with masonic phrases and oblique references which are apparent only to a Master Mason. Slight references also occur in *The Dog Harvey* (A Diversity of Creatures) and *The Wrong Thing* (Reward and Fairies). Whereas *The Janeites* a story of a Battery of Heavy Artillery in France during the First World War contains a most interesting masonic theme. There are also many other masonic references worked into his stories – In *Captains' Courageous*, Tom Platt reveals himself as a mason by what he describes to Harvey as 'sign talk'. In the curious story *.007* in *The Day's Work* the locomotives are made human and the running shed becomes a lodge room.

Henry Sadler Williamson in his excellent paper on Kipling refers to some works never published here but existing in American editions *Abaft the Funnel* and *The Enlightenments of Pagett MP* from which he selects that gem which cannot but strike a shaft into many a mason's conscience 'Here is Edwards, the Master of the Lodge I neglect so diligently'.

Kim, the story of a young Irish boy reared and nutured among the native children of an Indian city, is perhaps Kipling's masterpiece. Kim's father, a retired Colour Sergeant, went native after the death of his wife and became, alas, an habitual drunkard before he, too, died. In the estate left by the father, importance is attached to three papers he bequeathed his orphan son. The first of these was his MM's Diploma which he called 'Ne Varietur' because of the words below his signature: the other two were his Clearance Certificate from the lodge, and Kim's birth certificate. The influence of things masonic upon Kim's life is a theme woven skilfully throughout the narrative, with a hint of the ancient Eastern mysteries in the character of the old mendicant priest, in the search and travels of the Lama and mention of the mystic wheel.

A series of tales was written around the subject of a mythical lodge of instruction 'Lodge Faith and Works 5836' – *Fairy Kist, Madonna of the Trenches, A Friend of the Family*. The Grand

Lodge of Scotland Year Book in 1957 reprinted one of these tales *In the Interests of The Brethren*. There exists in the Library of the Grand Lodge of England a letter which was written to G. B. Fluke, Esq, from Brown's Hotel on 14 March 1919. It reads:

> Wo. Sir and Brother,
> I thank you very much for your kind letter and note what the Brethren are pleased to say about my tale called *In the Interests of the Brethren*. I am afraid it was rather presumption on my part to have written it as I have never passed the Chair and have held no rank higher than that of Secretary but, like yourself, I have heard visiting Brethren during the War, express their keen satisfaction wherever they found 'a cosy corner among the Brethren' at Lodge.
> Yours fraternally,
> RUDYARD KIPLING. MM

Masons will especially enjoy Kipling's *The Mother Lodge*, a poem which unambiguously declared the universal brotherhood of man. The subject is one of the cosmopolitan lodges common in India and the East, and the narrator purports to be a British soldier, good-hearted and well intentioned, with the beginnings of a dim consciousness of the grandeur and universality of the Craft. In this lodge of which he was Junior Deacon were several other British members, including the Master, a sergeant-major. The other nationalities and religions were represented by his 'Brethren black and brown' – Old Framjee, the piece goods importer, who was a Parsee and follower of Zoroaster; the Hindu Accountant, Bola Nath; Saul, the Jew from Aden; Din Mohammed, a Moslem; Babu Chuckerbutty, the Brahmin; the Sikh, Amir Singh; and the Eurasian half-caste, Castro, a Roman Catholic.

> An lookin' on it backwards
> It often strikes me thus,
> There ain't such things as infidels
> Except perhaps it's us.

After Labour they could not dine together 'lest a Brother's caste were broke', but gathered to smoke and talk of their respective religions until the time came to part.

> With Mohammed, God and Shiva
> changing pickets in our 'ead.

There they 'met upon the level and parted on the Square', brothers obligated to the same vows, enlightened by the Great Light of Masonry and animated by the same Fraternal principles.

> Outside – 'Sergeant!' 'Sir!' 'Salute'. 'Salaam'
> Inside – 'Brother' – an' it doesn't do no 'arm.

Many books and articles have been written on the subject of Kipling as a freemason. Students of masonic research would be most interested in one of the most comprehensive of these written by Albert Frost. Unfortunately this was for a limited circulation and it is hard to obtain. In his book Albert Frost refers to an interesting Toast List which was prepared for the annual gathering in 1929 of 'Hope and Perseverance Lodge' in Lahore. This is unique, as it contains all the usual toasts with appropriate extracts from one or other of Kipling's poems:

> *The King – Emperor and The Craft.*
> Robed, crowned and throned he weaves his spell.
> *The M.W. The Grand Master.*
> With him are the keys of the secret things.
> *The R.W., The D.G.M.'s and the D.G.L.*
> Keep ye the law, be swift in all obedience
> *The W.M. and his Officers*
> And they shall work for an age at a sitting
> and never be tired at all.
> *The I.P.M. and Outgoing Officers*
> We shall rest, and, faith we shall need it
> Lie down for an aeon or two,
> Till the Master of all Good Workmen
> Shall put us to work anew.
> *The Visiting Brethren.*
> Deeper than speech our love
> Stronger than life our Tether
> But we do not fall on their neck
> Nor kiss when we come together.

> *Punjab Masonic Charities*
> Help me to need no aid from men
> That I may help such men as need.
> *Absent Members*
> But I wish that I might meet them
> In my Mother Lodge once more.
> *The Non Masonic Guests.*
> The legion that never was listed
> Will send us as good as ourselves.
> *The Tyler*
> So it's knock out your pipe and follow me
> Follow me – follow me home.

What Kipling's exact position in the Temple of Fame may be is unimportant. What is certain is that his stories and poems of Anglo-Indian life and of the more mysterious and unfamiliar native life all palpitate with reality and actuality. He admits that his tales were collected from all sorts of people and places – from priests, medicants and fakirs, from nameless men on trains and steamers all over the world, from women spinning at their doors in the twilight, from officers and soldiers, 'but', he adds, 'the best were those my father gave me'. His works reveal a sense of realism, pathos and humour, welded by a deep and intense love of humanity, as becomes a good mason, and one cannot but be struck by his wise and brotherly toleration of the diverse creeds held by wise men of many lands.

> My brother kneels, so saith Kabir,
> To stone and brass in heathen-wise,
> But in my brother's voice I hear
> My own unanswered agonies.
> His God is as the fates assign
> His prayers are all the world's and mine.

And so, in spite of Kipling's humble characters, in spite of his somewhat too blatant jingoism, there is content in his writings, much that will survive all detraction and criticism. In them is found a true sincerity, a love of humanity and all that is best in human life and history, and over these qualities the viccissitudes of time and fashion have neither power nor sway.

To you is also recommended his fine short poems, *My New Cut Ashlar* and *Banquet Night*, which commences:

> Once in so often King Solomon said,
> Watching his quarrymen drill the stone,
> We will club our garlic and wine and bread
> And Banquet together beneath my throne
> And all the Brethren shall come to mess
> As Fellow-Craftsmen – no more and no less.

A beautiful masonic allegory is exemplified in another poem, *The Palace*, illustrating the realisation that we are all builders, and that each man contributes his part to that invisible temple not made with hands which humanity has sought to build through the ages. It is truth that no man finishes his work here, but, although the 'builders pass, the Building goes on eternally'.

Kipling died in 1936, and it is a recognition of the high esteem in which he was held that, after cremation, his ashes were placed in a grave next to Charles Dickens in the Poets' Corner in Westminster Abbey.

To us as men and Masons, Kipling has left behind much to attract, to be loved and valued, and to be kept like the acacia ever green in our thoughts and memories. Whether you are inspired to study his life and literature more intensely, or whether you are content to read and re-read a few favourite tales and poems, Kipling makes rewarding reading for the young mason who will readily seize on pointers to a wider comprehension of the spirit of brotherhood, and for Master Masons, who will rejoice to see the deep, inner truths that inspire many of his most noble phrases.

10
SIR WALTER SCOTT – FREEMASON

Adam M. Mackay

THE LODGE IN which Sir Walter Scott was initiated into freemasonry was constituted on 2 March 1738, under a Commission granted by the Right Honourable George, Earl of Cromarty, Grand Master Mason of the Grand Lodge of Scotland. The original name of the lodge, Canongate Kilwinning from Leith, was changed in 1756 to St David, at which it now remains, its present number on Grand Lodge Roll being 36.

The first meetings were held at the Laigh Coffee House, Canongate, Edinburgh. In 1745 the lodge removed to the convening House of the Corporation of Hammermen, also situated in the Canongate, and in 1753 to the Convening House of the Corporation of Cordiners, or Shoemakers, in the Potterrow Port. It was at this latter place that Walter Scott, WS, the father of the novelist, was made a mason.

In 1757 the brethren purchased a hall in Hyndford's Close, Netherbow, High Street, where the meetings were held for over a century. Other masonic bodies, including the Royal Order of Scotland, and the Royal Arch Chapter, now Edinburgh, No 1, held their earliest meetings there, and it was there that Sir Walter Scott and many other eminent Scotsmen were made freemasons.

The entry and stair leading to the lodge room was at the head of the close, on the west side, and was then a favourite residence. Sir Walter Scott's mother, Anne Rutherford, daughter of Dr John Rutherford, Professor of Medicine in the University of Edinburgh, passed her girlhood there, and Scott, when a lad, was often at his mother's old home, visiting his uncle, Dr Daniel Rutherford. Forty years afterwards Sir Walter, having occasion to correspond with Lady Anne Lindsay, authoress of the ballad of 'Auld Robin Gray', whose mother, Anne, Countess of Balcarres, had been a neighbour of the Rutherfords, told her:

> I remember all the locale of Hyndford's Close perfectly, even to the Indian screen of Harlequin and Columbine, and the harpsichord, though I never had the pleasure of hearing Lady Anne play upon it. I suppose the close, one too clean to soil the hem of your ladyship's garment, is now a resort for the lowest mechanics – and so wears the world away. . . . It is, to be sure, more picturesque to lament the desolation of towers on hills and haughs, than the degradation of an Edinburgh close; but I cannot help thinking on the simple and cosy retreats where worth and talent, and elegance to boot, were often nestled, and which now are the resort of misery, poverty and vice.

Notwithstanding the 'degradation' to which Sir Walter alludes, the lodge continued to meet at Hyndford's Close until the end of 1860. In 1838 the lodge room was repainted and redecorated by Brother David Ramsay Hay, one of the members. Brother Hay was distinguished for his efforts to raise the character of decorative painting, and for his writings on form and colour, and it was to him that Scott entrusted all the 'limning and blazoning' of the interior of Abbotsford.

From the date of its institution, Lodge St David was prosperous, and meetings were held regularly, with the exception of the period dating from June 1745 to December 1746, when the Right Worshipful Master considered it inadvisable to summon the members owing to the Jacobite Rebellion. The height of prosperity was reached in the session of 1754. Much of this prosperity was due to the influence of the Right Worshipful Master, Brother Walter Ferguson, a writer in Edinburgh, initiated in 1752. Brother Ferguson was owner of portions of the land on which the New Town of Edinburgh was built, including the whole of St James' Square. When the said Square was in process of building, the following incident is stated to have taken place between Sir Walter Scott's father and the Right Worshipful Master's son, Captain James Ferguson of the Royal Navy, initiated in 1753, when a Midshipman on the man-of-war *Success*. An attempt was being made to procure water by sinking wells for it, despite the elevation of the ground. Mr Scott happened one day to pass when Captain Ferguson was sinking a well of vast depth. Upon Scott expressing a doubt if water could be got there: 'I will get it', said the Captain, 'though I sink to hell for it!' 'A bad place for water', was the dry remark of the doubter.

The Fergusons and the Scotts were connected by marriage through the ancient border family of Swinton. 'A family', writes Sir Walter, 'which produced many distinguished warriors during the middle ages, and which, for antiquity and honourable alliances, may rank with any in Britain.'

Initiation of Scott's Father

Of those who were made masons in 1754, thirty are designated 'Writers', the profession to which the Right Worshipful Master belonged, and among them was Sir Walter Scott's father. He was initiated on 4 January, the first meeting held that session, and was recommended by the Right Worshipful Master, Brother Walter Ferguson. The following is an extract from the minute:

> The Lodge being convened on an Emergency . . . there was presented to the Lodge a Petition for Anthony Ferguson, Mercht. in Edinburgh, Walter Scott and John Tait, Writers in Edinburgh, craving to be made Masons and admitted Members of this Lodge, and being recommended by the Right Worshipful Master, the Desire of their Petition was unanimously granted and they were accordingly made Masons, and each paid his full Dues to the Treasurer. . . .

Brother Scott was born on 11 May 1729, and was the eldest son of Robert Scott, farmer at Sandy Knowe, in the vicinity of Smailholm Tower, Roxburghshire, a descendant of Sir Walter

Scott, of Harden. The Scotts of Harden, again came, in the fourteenth century from the stock of the Buccleuchs. He was educated for the profession of Writer to the Signet, to which Society he was admitted in 1755. 'Through his family connection he obtained a good practice, which partly owing to his punctilious manner, subsequently decreased. Singularly conscientious, he would, according to Sir Walter, have sacrificed his own interest to that of his client, and though economical to the verge of penury, would, in carrying out any duties entrusted to him, have been content to suffer loss.'

His portrait is drawn for us by his son, under the disguise of Saunders Fairford in *Redgauntlet.*

Brother Scott stepped quickly into prominence in the lodge, and before receiving the second Degree, acted as Junior Warden, in the absence of that official, on 25 and 30 January, and also on 4 February. On 20 March he was passed Fellow-of-Craft, and two days later was raised to the Degree of Master Mason. He again acted as Junior Warden, *pro tempore*, on 29 March and 3 April, and on 10 April as Deputy Master. At the Festival of St John the Evangelist, 27 December 1754, within a year of his initiation, he was elected and installed Senior Warden. The minutes of the meetings at this period were signed by the Right Worshipful Master and Wardens, and Brother Scott's signature, as Junior Warden, *pro tempore*, 1754, and as Senior Warden in 1755, appears in the Minute Book nineteen times.

For many years after the institution of the lodge it was customary to select what was termed a 'leet' of three brethren for the office of Right Worshipful Master, their names being submitted and a vote taken, if necessary, at the Annual Festival on winter St John's day. Scott was nominated one of the leet for the Mastership, at a meeting held on 10 December 1755. The minute states that:

> '. . . The Rt. Worshipfull' (Bro. James Ewart, Accountant, Royal Bank), 'proposed the Worshipful Bro. James Walker Dt. Mr. for one' (of the leet) 'which the Lodge unanimously agreed to. The Wardens' (Bros. Walter Scott and John Gray) 'proposed the Rt. Worshipfull himself for another. And the Brethren of the Lodge

named the Worshipfull Brother Walter Scott Senior Warden for the third. All the three being unanimously approved of by the Members. . . .'

At the Annual Festival on 27 December the brethren unanimously agreed to the election of the Right Worshipful Master's nominee, and the Deputy Master, Brother James Walker, physician, was installed in the Chair.

The next record of interest in connection with Sir Walter Scott's father occurs thirty years afterwards, on 7 December 1785, when, in the absence of the Right Worshipful Master he occupied the Chair.

The Brethren being convened, Br. Walter Scott, Esqr. took the Chair and the Lodge being regularly opened and constituted, a petition was presented for Messrs Robert Scott, Chicherter Cheyne (both sailors) and John Johnston Craving to be made Masons and Members of this Lodge; and the two former, viz.: – Messrs Scott & Cheyne being recommended by the R.W. Br. Scott, and Mr Johnston by Br. Wm. Allan the desire of the petition was unanimously granted, and by direction from the chair the Ceremony was performed by Br. Paterson. . . .'

This Minute is signed 'Walter Scott'.

Sir Walter Scott's Brother

The two sailors recommended by Brother Scott would, in all probability, be of some social standing and it is quite possible that the Robert Scott referred to was Sir Walter's elder brother. He retired from the naval service after the peace of Paris (Versailles, 1783) and would likely be staying at home at this period. It is quite possible that this meeting was held specially at the request of Brother Scott for the purpose of initiating his son and Mr Cheyne.

'My eldest brother (that is, the eldest whom I remember to have seen) was Robert Scott, . . . He was bred in the King's service, under Admiral, then Captain William Dickson, and was in most of *Rodney*'s battles. His temper was bold and haughty, and to me was often checkered with what I felt to be capricious tyranny. In other respects I loved him much, for he had a strong turn for literature, read poetry with taste and judgment, and composed verses himself which had gained him great applause among his messmates. Witness the following elegy upon the supposed loss of the vessel, composed the night before *Rodney*'s celebrated battle of the 12th April 1782. It alludes to the various amusements of his mess:

> No more the geese shall cackle on the poop,
> No more the bagpipe through the orlop sound,
> No more the midshipmen, a jovial group,
> Shall toast the girls, and push the bottle round.
> In death's dark road at anchor fast they stay,
> Till Heaven's loud signal shall in thunder roar,
> Then starting up, all hands shall quick obey,
> Sheet home the topsail, and with speed unmoor'.

Robert sang agreeably – (a virtue which was never seen in me) – understood the mechanical arts, and when in good humour could regale us with many a tale of bold adventure and narrow escapes. When in bad humour, however, he gave us a practical taste of what was then man-of-war's discipline, and kicked and cuffed without mercy. I have often thought how he might have distinguished himself had he continued in the navy until the present times, so glorious for nautical exploit. But the Peace of Paris cut off all hopes of promotion for those who had not great interest; and some disgust, which his proud spirit had taken at harsh usage from a superior officer, combined to throw poor Robert into the East India Company's service, for which his habits were ill adapted. He made two voyages to the East, and died a victim to the climate. . . .

Subsequent to 7 December 1785, there is no further reference in the lodge minutes to Sir Walter Scott's father.

> The death of this worthy man, in his 70th year, after a long series of feeble health and suffering, was an event which could only be regarded as a great deliverance to himself. He had had a succession of paralytic attacks, under which mind as well as body had by degrees been laid quite prostrate.

He died on 13 April 1799 and was buried in the Greyfriars Churchyard, Edinburgh. At the left-hand entrance to the iron door immediately to the west of New Greyfriars Church there is a granite memorial, interesting from its unique brevity and national importance:

> IN FRONT OF THIS TABLET
> LIE THE REMAINS
> OF
> WALTER SCOTT, ESQUIRE, W.S.
> FATHER OF
> SIR WALTER SCOTT
> WITH THOSE OF SEVERAL MEMBERS OF THE SAME FAMILY.

Sir Walter Scott Initiated

Sir Walter Scott when initiated into freemasonry was thirty years of age. He was born in the College Wynd, Edinburgh, on 15 August 1771, and was educated at the High School. Previous to entering the University, in November 1783, he spent some weeks in Kelso, where he attended daily the public school. It was there that he became acquainted with the brothers James and John Ballantyne, with whom he subsequently entered into partnership in the printing and publishing business of Ballantyne & Co. In his fifteenth year he was indentured as an apprentice to his father. On the expiry of his apprenticeship in 1790, he resolved to follow another branch of the legal profession; and having passed through the usual studies, was admitted, in 1792, a member of the Faculty of Advocates. On 16 December 1799 he was appointed to the Sheriffdom of Selkirkshire, and in the same month married Charlotte Margaret Carpenter, daughter of John Carpenter of Lyons.

At an Emergency Meeting, held on Monday, 2 March 1801, Walter Scott was initiated, passed and raised in Lodge St David. The minute of this meeting does not give the name of his proposer, but doubtless the fact of his father having been long and intimately connected with the lodge was an inducement to him to join it. There were also other reasons which may have influenced him. The Most Worshipful Grand Master in 1801, The Earl of Dalkeith, afterwards Charles, Duke of Buccleuch, who claimed 'St David's' as his Mother Lodge, 'had been participating in the military patriotism of the period, and had been thrown into Scott's society under circumstances well qualified to ripen acquaintance into confidence.' The brothers James and John Ballantyne also were frequent attenders at the lodge, and Scott had been brought much into contact with them in connection with the publishing of the *Minstrelsy of the Scottish Border*, the first two volumes of which were issued from the Kelso Press in January 1802. The following extract from a minute of meeting held on 18 March 1800, is interesting:

> ... It ought not to be passed over how much was contributed to the entertainment of the Lodge by Brethren Ballantyne of the Kelso Lodge to whose social dispositions, elegant manners and musical powers the Lodge of St David's are no strangers. The R.W. Master called on the Brethren to drink to the health of these two respectable visitors, particularly to that of Brother James Ballantyne who had formerly been . . . of this Lodge and who now held the office of . . . in the Kelso Lodge. . . . The toast was drunk with the greatest possible applause and was returned in a handsome and appropriate address from Mr James Ballantyne.

There is no reference in the records to the office held by Brother James Ballantyne in the Lodge. He was Right Worshipful Master of Lodge 'Kelso', Kelso, now No 58, in 1802, and in August 1814, was appointed representative of that lodge at the meetings of the Grand Lodge in Edinburgh. He has been described as a kind-hearted and talented man, a good critic and a friend highly esteemed by Scott. His brother John's aptitude for business has been seriously questioned; he was manager of the printing establishment. In the jovial, literary and artistic society which he frequented, his racy humour and endless stories never failed to be appreciated.

It was on Scott's suggestion that the Ballantynes settled in Edinburgh to engage in the printing business. A letter sent by Scott to James Ballantyne refers to that matter. It is also interesting from the fact that it makes reference to another acquaintance of Scott's, Brother Joseph Gillon, a member of Lodge St David, and Right Worshipful Master in 1805–6 and 7.

To MR J. BALLANTYNE,
    Kelso Mail OFFICE, KELSO,
    CASTLE STREET, *22nd April 1800.*

DEAR SIR,
 I am still resolved to have recourse to your press for the Ballads of the Border, which are in some forwardness.

 I have now to request your forgiveness for mentioning a plan which your friend Gillon and I have talked over with a view as well to the public advantage as to your individual interest. It is nothing short of a migration from Kelso to this place. . . .

 Three branches of printing are quite open in Edinburgh, all of which I am convinced you have both the ability and inclination to unite in your person. . . .

 It appears to me that such a plan, judiciously adopted and diligently pursued, opens a fair road to an ample fortune. In the meanwhile the *Kelso Mail* might be so arranged as to be still a source of some advantage to you; and I dare say, if wanted, pecuniary assistance might be procured to assist you at the outset, either upon terms of a share or otherwise; but I refer you for particulars to Joseph, in whose room I am now assuming the pen, for reasons too distressing to be declared, but at which you will readily guess. I hope, at all events, you will impute my interference to anything rather than an impertinent intermeddling with your concerns on the part of, dear Sir,
    Your obedient servant,
        WALTER SCOTT.

The Joseph Gillon here named was a solicitor of some eminence, a man of strong abilities and genuine wit and humour, for whom Scott, as well as Ballantyne, had a warm regard. Calling on him one day at his office, Scott said, 'Why, Joseph, this place is as hot as an oven.' 'Well', said Gillon, 'and isn't it here that I make my bread?' He was initiated on 21 January 1800, and was the same evening appointed secretary of the lodge, was Junior Warden in 1801, and Depute Master in 1802 and 1803. He became Right Worshipful Master in 1805, from which position he retired on 24 June 1808. The intemperate habits alluded to at the close of Scott's letter gradually undermined his business, his health and his character; and he was glad, on leaving Edinburgh some years afterwards, to obtain a humble situation about the House of Lords. Scott, casually meeting him on one of his visits to London, expressed his regret at having lost his society in Edinburgh; Joseph responded by a quotation from the Scotch Metrical Version of the Psalm:

> 'rather in
> The Lord's house would I keep a door
> Than dwell in the tents of sin.'

The Right Worshipful Master of Lodge St David in the year of Sir Walter Scott's initiation, was Brother Houston Rigg Brown, of Messrs Brown & Company, Coachmakers, Abbey Hill, Edinburgh. He was initiated in 1795, and held the office of Right Worshipful Master from 1800 to 1804. On 24 June 1808 he was re-elected to the Chair, on the resignation of Brother Joseph Gillon, and continued as Right Worshipful Master until the end of 1819. He took great interest in the affairs of the lodge, and twenty years after leaving the Chair, on 12 November 1839, was entertained by the brethren at a Masonic Festival held in his honour.

Three Degrees at one Meeting

The minute of the Emergency Meeting held on Monday, 2 March 1801, reads as follows:

> There having been many applications for entries in the Lodge, the present evening was appointed for that purpose, when the following Gentlemen were admitted apprentices, Andrew Ross, George McKattie, Walter Scott, John Campbell. The Lodge was afterwards successively opened as a Fellow Craft's and Master's Lodge when the following Brethren were passed, and raised to the degrees of Master Masons, vizt., The said Andrew Ross, George McKattie, Walter Scott, as also John Tod, James Luke, George Morse, Hugh McLean, William Dunlop, Lieut. George Pott, Lieut. George Dunlop, Patrick Erskine, James Hope, Bruce Robt. Nairne, John Ramsay, Alexr. Kedie, David Anderson, James Dewar, Robert Walker. The ceremony was gone through on this occasion with very great accuracy and solemnity by the Right

Worshipful Master, who afterwards took the chair. And the Lodge being joined by some of the other brethren, continued together for some time in the usual amusements of the Craft. It may be here added, that from the institution of the Lodge of St Davids to this present time, there has not been an instance of so great a number being on one occasion entered masons.

J. CAMPBELL, Secy

The last paragraph in the minute is misleading, and would have been more correct if it had stated that there had not been an instance of so great a number being on one occasion passed and raised. Sir Walter Scott's name is recorded in the books of the Grand Lodge of Scotland under date, 31 July 1802. The recording of the names of entrants appears to have been very irregular at this period, the list previous to that containing Scott's name being sent in to Grand Lodge in 1790.

The next record of interest in connection with Sir Walter is a minute of meeting, held a year later, and summoned at his special request. It is dated 23 March 1802:

> At the desire of Walter Scott, Esq., Advocate, a meeting of a few of the Brethren was called to be present at the entry of a Gentleman from England, Dewhurst Bilsborrow of Dalby house. He was in common form duly admitted apprentice, passed Fellow Craft and raised to the degree of Master Mason. At the entry of this Brother a good deal of new apparatus was procured, which added very much to the solemnity of the occasion.

No reference is made in the minutes during Scott's lifetime to his being again present at any of the meetings of the lodge. Unfortunately, the minute book following that in which his initiation is recorded, dating from 27 December 1807 to 21 December 1832, was very badly kept, there being many blanks in the volume, the most serious extending from December 1814 to December 1820. The unfortunate differences with the Grand Lodge of Scotland during the years 1807 to 1813, which resulted in the temporary secession from that body of several of the lodges in Edinburgh, including Lodge St David, was partly the cause of this, a subsequent minute stating that 'the book was so long in the hands of the Grand Lodge having the legal minutes engrossed . . . .'.

Proposed Change of Lodge Name

An interesting reference to Scott having frequently attended the meetings was made in 1841, when a motion was submitted by the secretary, Brother John D. Douglas, to change the name 'St David' to 'Sir Walter Scott's Lodge'. Speaking in favour of the Change, the Secretary said:

> . . . The circumstances of his father (Walter Scott, W.S.) being a very zealous member, as well as Office-bearer would almost account for his choice of this particular Lodge, independent of the reputation which it at that time, and has ever since enjoyed. He seemed to have entered considerably into the spirit of the meetings, by attending them frequently and in bringing forward members to be initiated. It is unfortunate, however, that the records were so slovenly compiled at that time and for many years after as to prevent us now from ascertaining the actual part he took in promoting the prosperity of the Lodge, but I am credibly informed that he was often called on to add his mite to the harmony of the evening, when he would electrify his audience by some quaint story illustrating the character and customs of his countrymen, or by the powers of his wit and humour shedding around him a halo of pleasure which there was no man of his day more capable of doing . . .

The motion to change the name of the lodge was defeated by a majority. Several of the older members were present and took part in the discussion, among others being Brother Alexander Deuchar of Morningside, initiated in St David's in May 1801, two months after Scott was made a Mason. Brother Deuchar was Right Worshipful Master of the Lodge of Edinburgh, Mary's Chapel, No 1, during the years 1810 to 1814, 1824–5 and 1834. He published a work on heraldry, which he dedicated to Sir Walter.

Scott's Literary Works

In 1805 Scott's first great work, the *Lay of the Last Minstrel*, was published. The poem of *Marmion* appeared in 1808, and the *Lady of the Lake* in 1810. In 1805 also, about seven chapters of the story of *Waverley* had been written, but, discouraged by one of his critical friends, to whom he had shown the manuscript, Scott threw the work aside. Accidentally coming across the fragment in 1814, he completed it in three weeks, and in July of the same year it was given anonymously to the public. In rapid succession the other novels were written, and no fewer than eighteen, comprising about sixty volumes, appeared in eleven years. The second, *Guy Mannering*, appeared in 1815, and in 1816 followed *The Antiquary* and the first series of the *Tales of my Landlord*.

On 4 June of this year Scott, in the absence of the Provincial Grand Master of the District, the Most Noble the Marquis of Lothian, laid the foundation stone of a new lodge room at Selkirk, and was elected an Honorary Member of the lodge there, 'St John', now No 32 on Grand Lodge Roll. The following appears in the records of that Lodge:

> June 4, 1816, This being the day appointed for Laying the Foundation Stone of the Free Masons hall, a most numerous meeting of the Brethren, along with a respectable deputation from Hawick and visiting Brethren from Peebles and Jedburgh went in procession according to the order of Procession inserted on the 143rd and 144th page hereof, when the stone was laid by Walter Scott Esquire of Abbotsford Sheriff Depute of the County of Selkirk, who, after making a most eloquent and appropriate Speech, Deposited in the Stone the different Coins of his Majesty's Reign, with the Newspapers of the day, and the Inscription as inserted on the 145th page hereof. The Revd. Mr James Nicol of Traquair gave an excellent prayer well adapted for the occasion. After the ceremony of laying the Stone was over the Brethren returned to the Town hall, and on the motion of Brother Walter Hogg the unanimous thanks of the Brethren was voted to Mr Scott for the honour he had conferred upon the Lodge by his presence and laying the Foundation Stone. On the motion of Brother Andrew Lang the unanimous thanks of the Brethren was also voted to the Revd. Mr Nicol for the obliging manner he had consented to come to this place to act as Chaplain and for his conduct throughout. On the motion of Brother James Robertson, Mr Scott was admitted an Honorary Member with three Cheers.
>
> The meeting then walked to Mr Minto's Inn where they dined, and spent the evening with the utmost conviviality, Mr Scott filling the Chair to the satisfaction of all present.

The inscription deposited in the stone was as follows:

E.D.O.M.
WALTER SCOTT ESQUIRE OF ABBOTSFORD
SHERIFF DEPUTE OF SELKIRKSHIRE
LAID
THIS FOUNDATION STONE
OF THE FREE MASON'S HALL
SELKIRK
UPON THE 4TH DAY OF JUNE
IN THE YEAR OF OUR LORD 1816
AND THE REIGN OF G. III. K OF GREAT BRITAIN
56TH YEAR
AND OF THE ERA OF MASONRY 5816
JAMES INGLIS AND DAVID LAIDLAW
CONTRACTORS OF THE WORK
Q.D.B.V.

Writing next day to the Duke of Buccleuch, the Grand Master of 1801–2, Scott made reference to the laying of the foundation stone in the following terms:

ABBOTSFORD, *June 5th, 1816.*

MY DEAR LORD,
 . . . I was under the necessity of accepting the honour done me by the Souters, who requested me to lay the foundation stone of a sort of barn which is to be called a Free Masons Hall. There was a solemn procession on this occasion, which, that it might not want the decorum of costume, was attended by weavers from Hawick, shoemakers from Jedburgh, and pedlars from Peebles, all very fine in the scarfs and trinkums of their respective lodges. If our musical band was not complete, it was at least varied, for besides the town drum and fife, which thundered in the van, we had a pair of bagpipes and two fiddles, and we had a prayer from a parson whom they were obliged to initiate on the spur of the occasion, who was abominably frightened, although I assured him the sanctity of his cloth would preserve him from the fate of the youngest brother alluded to by Burns in his 'Address to the Deil' . . .

Believe me, my dear Lord Duke, ever your truly honoured and obliged

WALTER SCOTT.

Subsequent to the laying of the foundation stone at Selkirk, no records of importance have been brought to light in connection with Sir Walter and the Order. The Lodge of Melrose, No 1, possesses two letters written by him conveying apologies for inability to attend certain meetings, one undated, and the other written in 1825, being his declinature to lay the foundation stone of the Chain Bridge across the Tweed at Melrose.

The announcement of Scott having been made a Baronet appeared in the gazette of 1 April 1820. Sir Walter was the first Baronet created by King George IV.

On 16 June 1821 Lodge St John, No 111, Hawick, held a meeting to 'consider the propriety of a public procession at laying the foundation stone of a sett of Subscription Rooms about to be built in Hawick. The minute book of that lodge contains the following entry:

'A deputation was appointed to wait upon Sir Walter Scott of Abbotsford, at his country seat, to request the honour of his company at the approaching festival, and to preside upon the occasion.'

Sir Walter does not appear to have accepted the invitation of the Hawick Brethren.

Failure of Printing Business

The failure of the printing business of Ballantyne & Co. took place in 1826. Scott's liabilities as a partner amounted to nearly £150,000. Determined that his creditors should be paid to the last farthing, he refused to be a party to a composition or to accept of any discharge. He pledged himself to devote the whole labour of his subsequent life to the payment of his debts, and he fulfilled the pledge. In the course of four years his works yielded nearly £70,000, and, ultimately, his creditors received every farthing of their claims. This arduous labour cost him much. In February 1830 he had an attack of an apoplectic nature, from which he never thoroughly recovered. After another severe shock in April 1831 he was at length persuaded to abandon literary work. At Abbotsford, on 21 September 1832, in the sixty-second year of his age, he died, surrounded by his family and with the murmur of the Tweed in his ears. Five days later the remains of Sir Walter Scott were laid in the sepulchre of his ancestors in the old Abbey of Dryburgh.

An invitation to attend the celebration of the First Centenary of Lodge St David, held on 19 February 1839, was sent to Sir Walter's eldest son, the Second Baronet of Abbotsford, then Lieutenant-Colonel of the 15th Dragoons. The minute book states:

> The following was directed by the Committee to be sent to Br. Sir Walter Scott, Bart., presently in town. At a meeting of the Committee of the Lodge Edinr. Saint David held this day, (9th Feb.) in consideration of our illustrious and lamented Brother the late Sir Walter Scott having been made a Mason in this Lodge and having a high respect for his Son Brother Sir Walter Scott presently residing in Edinburgh, it was unanimously resolved to intimate to that Brother that a Convivial Meeting of this Lodge would be held here on Tuesday, the 19th instant at 8 o'clock evening, in Commemoration of the Centenary of the Lodge and respectfully to request the honour of his company on that occasion. The Committee accordingly appointed the R.W. Sub. Master Brother J. B. Douglas and the Secretary of the Lodge Bro. J. D. Douglas to wait on Brother Sir W. Scott to receive his answer.

There is no record of his having been present at the centenary meeting, and it is to be regretted that the foregoing extract does not mention the lodge to which he belonged. This year, 1839, he proceeded to India with his regiment, which he subsequently commanded. At Bangalore, in 1846, he was smitten with fever, culminating in liver disease. Having sailed for home, he died on board the ship *Wellesley*, near the Cape of Good Hope, on 8 February 1847, aged forty-six.

Walter Scott Lockhart, younger son of John Gibson Lockhart and Sophia, elder daughter of the novelist, succeeded to the estate of Abbotsford on the death of his uncle, and assumed the name and arms of Scott. He was a Lieutenant in the 16th Lancers, and was a member of Lodge Canongate Kilwinning, No 2, Edinburgh. He died at Versailles on 10 January 1853.

Lodge St David subscribed towards the erection of the

monument to Sir Walter Scott, in Princes Street, Edinburgh, and was present, on 15 August 1840, at the laying of the foundation stone of that structure by the Grand Master Mason, Sir James Forrest of Comiston, Lord Provost of the City. A detailed account of the proceedings, is engrossed in the Lodge Minute Book, including the following paragraph:

> By kind permission of the Right W. Master (Bro. John Donaldson Boswall of Wardie, Captain R.N.) as Deputy Governor of the Royal Order of Scotland, and the other members present, the Brethren belonging to St David's Lodge were allowed the use of the ancient and beautiful Jewels, as well as crimson Sash belonging to the Order. The phœnix Society of Tailors also sent their Sashes in terms of their kind offer detailed in the Minute of the 28th July last, so that every member who joined the Lodge in Procession was clothed in a Green and Crimson Sash, the first over the right and the second over the left shoulder.

The lodge was also present at the inauguration of the monument on 15 August 1846. New clothing was obtained for the occasion, and a new Banner unfurled for the first time, having on the one side the inscription:

'ST DAVID'S LODGE
SIR WALTER SCOTT, BART.
INITIATED
2ND MARCH 1801

and on the other:

INAUGURATION OF THE SCOTT MONUMENT
15TH AUGUST 1846

Reprinted by kind permission from Volume XX of Ars Quatuor Coronatorum, The Transactions of the Quatuor Coronati Lodge, No 2076 E.C.

11

LODGE MOTHER KILWINNING No 0

George Draffen

IT IS IMPOSSIBLE within the compass of a few pages to do more than trace in outline the rise and progress of this venerable old lodge. Lodge Mother Kilwinning still awaits a historian of the calibre of Murray Lyon or R. S. Lindsay who will deal as faithfully with her history as they have done for the Lodge of Edinburgh (Mary's Chapel) and the Lodge of Holyrood House (St Luke). Three histories of Lodge Mother Kilwinning have been written. Lee Ker and Robert Wylie published theirs in book form. That by Murray Lyon appeared as a serial in the long defunct 'Scottish Freemason's Magazine'. All three were members of the lodge and all three should be read if one is to obtain any sound knowledge of the lodge which stands so proudly at the head of the Scottish Roll.

The origin of the lodge is uncertain, although it most probably began with the building of the monastery at Kilwinning. Whatever its beginnings, by 1598 it had become one of three lodges mentioned in the *Schaw Statutes* of that year. These Statutes, and a further set issued in 1599, were promulgated by William Schaw, Master of the King's Masons and were compiled for the better administration of operative building in Scotland.

The order of seniority assigned in these Statutes to the three lodges at Edinburgh, Kilwinning and Stirling has aroused considerable controversy. Had the existence of these Statutes been known in 1736 it is just possible that Mother Kilwinning would not have withdrawn, in 1743, from the Grand Lodge of Scotland at whose birth she was represented. It was not until some years after 1736 that the Grand Lodge of Scotland assigned any seniority to the lodges on the roll. Such seniority was based upon records which could be produced as evidence of antiquity. Here Mother Kilwinning was at a disadvantage, for her written minutes did not commence until 1641 and the existence of the *Schaw Statutes* with their evidence of her existence were unknown. As a consequence, the lodge was placed second on the roll of Grand Lodge – a position which the lodge resented and declined to accept. The lodge based its claim for precedence upon the fact that earlier records than 1641 had been consumed by a fire which had destroyed the family seat of the Earls of Eglinton wherein they were stored.

Finding Grand Lodge unpersuaded as to her claim to the prior position on the roll, Mother Kilwinning withdrew her allegiance and resumed her independence and powers of granting Charters. It is open to doubt whether in joining Grand Lodge, she had ever surrendered her chartering powers, though one might reasonably assume that, by the fact of adhering to Grand Lodge, she had done so.

That Mother Kilwinning had exercised the power of granting Charters before 1736 is not in doubt. Lodge Canongate Kilwinning was chartered by Mother Kilwinning in 1677 and St John's Lodge at Inverness within a few years thereafter at the least. The lodge at Duns, in Berwickshire, also appears to have been issued with a Kilwinning Charter before 1736.

Between 1743 and 1807, when she rejoined Grand Lodge, Mother Kilwinning continued to function as a Sovereign Grand Lodge, completely ignoring and being ignored by, the Grand Lodge of Scotland. During this period in her history she issued approximately seventy Charters, both within Scotland and overseas.

Unfortunately Mother Kilwinning was not blessed with very competent secretaries, for the record of the issue of her Charters is very incomplete. One must remember, too, that the situation of the lodge, in a small village in Ayrshire, can hardly have been conducive to the easy conduct of the business of a Grand Lodge. Travelling was difficult and the postal services, if they existed, cannot have been other than erratic.

The independence of Mother Kilwinning, at least during the early years of the period 1743–1807, does not seem to have brought with it any unfraternal feelings to Grand Lodge or her subordinate lodges. At least one Grand Master Mason was a member of Mother Kilwinning and Grand Lodge placed no ban on her members visiting Daughter Lodges of Mother Kilwinning – that was to come later.

Mention has been made above that Mother Kilwinning issued Charters outwith as well as within Scotland. One of these charters was issued on 8 October 1779 to the 'High Knight Templar of Ireland Kilwinning' Lodge, meeting in Dublin. The existence of this Charter has done much to support the completely erroneous idea that Lodge Mother Kilwinning worked masonic degrees other than the three degrees of St John's Masonry. Early in the eighteenth century there arose the idea that in Scotland in general, and in Lodge Mother Kilwinning in particular, there existed a body of High Degree Masons. The origin of this idea is not known, but it persisted until almost the close of the nineteenth century – and indeed the theory may still be cherished in some quarters. The degrees attributed to Mother Kilwinning were countless, but the most diligent search in her archives by Murray Lyon failed to reveal any reference to degrees other than those which are worked in Craft Lodges the world over. Not even an early record of the Mark Degree has been found. That such records may have existed and been destroyed about 1807 is not impossible, but, if this is so, the destruction has been so complete that not a vestige remains.

From 1743 onwards Mother Kilwinning and the Grand Lodge of Scotland seem to have pursued parallel, but independent, paths in fraternal accord. Both issued Charters and the difficulties of travel would doubtless prevent much intervisitation between subordinate lodges of the different allegiances. Such a state of affairs could not be expected to continue indefinitely. The Grand Lodge of Scotland grew rapidly. Mother Kilwinning's jurisdiction grew but slowly. Toward the end of the eighteenth century Grand Lodge prohibited her members from visiting Kilwinning Lodges and forbade her lodges from receiving Kilwinning Masons as visitors. Mother Kilwinning began to receive letters from her Daughter Lodges protesting at this state of affairs, but there was nothing she could do in the matter beyond advising a dignified silence and instructing her lodges to 'keep themselves to themselves'. Not a few of the Kilwinning Lodges came under Grand Lodge from time to time and it soon became clear that Mother Kilwinning's days as an independent Sovereign Grand Lodge were numbered. By 1807 only six of her lodges, all within Scotland, remained outwith Grand Lodge.

The first move in re-uniting Mother Kilwinning to Grand Lodge came from the latter body who wrote that 'the cause of the separation seemed to be forgotten', and suggested that Mother Kilwinning and her Daughter Lodges might come in to Grand Lodge on terms to be agreed. To this suggestion Mother Kilwinning concurred and, after some negotiations, the following terms were signed on behalf of both parties:

At Glasgow, the 14th day of October 1807.

At a meeting of the Committees appointed by the Grand Lodge of Scotland and the Mother Lodge of Kilwinning, vested by their respective constituents with full powers for the adjustment of their Masonic differences:

Present on the part of the Grand Lodge – William Inglis, Esq., Substitute Grand Master; Sir John Stewart, Bart., of Allanbank; Alexander Laurie, Esq.; Wm. Guthrie, Esq., Grand Secretary; and James Bartram, Esq., Grand Clerk.

And on the part of the Mother Lodge Kilwinning – William Blair, Esq., of Blair, Master; Robert Davidson, Esq., of Drumley, Depute Master; Alex. McGowan, Esq., of Smithson, Senior Warden; Alexander Hamilton, Esq., of Grange; Robt. Montgomerie, Esq., of Craighouse; and James Crichton, Esq., Collector of his Majesty's Customs, Irvine.

The Committee having exhibited and exchanged their respective powers, and carefully considered the matters in dispute, reciprocally agree as follows:

1st. That the Mother Lodge, Kilwinning, shall renounce all right of granting Charters, and come in, along with all the Lodges holding under her, to the bosom of the Grand Lodge.

2dly. That all the Lodges holding of Mother Kilwinning shall be obliged to obtain from the Grand Lodge confirmations of their respective Charters, for which a fee of three guineas only shall be exigible.

3dly. That the Mother Kilwinning shall be placed at the head of the Roll of the Grand Lodge, under the denomination of Mother Kilwinning; and her Daughter Lodges shall, in the meantime, be placed at the end of the said Roll, and as they shall apply for confirmations; but under this express declaration, that as soon as the Roll shall be arranged and corrected, which is in present contemplation, the Lodges holding of Mother Kilwinning shall be entitled to be ranked according to the dates of their original Charters, and of those granted by the Grand Lodge.

4thly. That Mother Kilwinning and her Daughter Lodges shall have the same interest in and management of the funds of the Grand Lodge, as the other Lodges now holding of her, – Mother Lodge, Kilwinning, contributing annually to the said funds a sum not less that two shillings and sixpence for each intrant, and her Daughter lodges contributing in the same manner as the present Lodges holding of the Grand Lodge.

5thly. That the Master of the Mother Lodge, Kilwinning, for the time, shall by *ipso facto* Provincial Grand Master for the Ayrshire District. And,

Lastly. While both Committees are satisfied that the preceding arrangement will be highly conducive to the honour and interest of Scottish Masonry, and though vested with the fullest powers to make a final adjustment, the Committee do only respectfully recommend its adoption to their respective constituents.

WILLIAM INGLIS, S.G.M.	WILL BLAIR.
JO. STEWART.	ROBT. DAVIDSON.
ALEX. LAURIE.	ROBT. MONTGOMERIE.
WM. GUTHRIE, Gd. Secy.	ALEX. MCGOWN.
JA. BARTRAM, Gd. Clk.	ALEX. HAMILTON.
	JAMES CRICHTON.

With the return of Mother Kilwinning to Grand Lodge it was necessary to re-arrange the Roll of Lodges and Mother Kilwinning was placed at the head, her subordinate lodges occupying positions in accordance with the dates of their

Kilwinning Charters. To this arrangement the Lodge of Edinburgh (Mary's Chapel) raised objection, but the matter was allowed to rest in the interests of fraternal peace. The terms of the agreement between Mother Kilwinning and Grand Lodge were, in the early years after the re-union, the subject of minor contentions between the two parties. The particular clause which seemed to engender most dispute was that which provided for the Master of Mother Kilwinning being *ex officio* Provincial Grand Master of Ayrshire. A desire by Grand Lodge to divide Ayrshire into two provinces (North and South) was frustrated by the lodge declining to recognise such a partition. (Ayr North was to have the Master of Mother Kilwinning as its Provincial Grand Master.) None of these disputes came to anything and Mother Kilwinning has remained an honoured member of Grand Lodge these last hundred and forty odd years.

It may be added that although the name 'Kilwinning' appears in the title of a large number of Scottish lodges, it most generally indicates an affection for an old lodge rather than any actual connection with it.

Many famous names are connected with Lodge Mother Kilwinning and her Daughter Lodges. The present Master, the 17th Earl of Eglington, perpetuates the close connection between the lodge and the family of Montgomerie. Many other distinguished brethren who have been admitted to membership of Lodge Mother Kilwinning include the Earl of Crawfurd, the Earl of Cassillis, Lord Lyle, etc. Mother Kilwinning's daughters have also initiated some famous men. Robert Burns was a member of Tarbolton Kilwinning, several of whose minutes bear the holograph of 'Robert Burnesse, Depute-Master'. General Sir John Moore, who is buried at Corunna, was initiated in Lodge Renfrew County Kilwinning – a lodge still on the Roll of Grand Lodge.

12

A MISSING GRAND MASTER MASON
HRH The Prince of Wales – HM King George IV

H. V. de Lorey

BROWSING AMONG OLD books is always a fascinating and sometimes a rewarding experience and browsing among the books in the Grand Lodge Library proved to be no exception when looking for clues to the choice of the name 'Union' for a Lodge (No 244) which celebrated its 150th anniversary on 4 May 1962.

It did not take long to discover that Union was very much in the air in masonic circles in the early years of the nineteenth century. Having hitherto been in fraternal relationship only with the Grand Lodge of England (Ancients), the Grand Lodge of Scotland, in 1805, entered into fraternal union with the Grand Lodge of England (Moderns). More important still, the year 1813 saw the union of these two Grand Lodges in England to form what is now the United Grand Lodge of England. When this union took place three Royal Brothers were at the head of Masonry in the three Grand Lodges – namely HRH The Prince of Wales and Prince Regent (later HM King George IV) as Grand Master Mason of Scotland; HRH the Duke of Kent as Grand Master of the Grand Lodge of England according to the Old Institutions; and HRH the Duke of Sussex as Grand Master of the Grand Lodge of England (Moderns).

A MISSING GRAND MASTER MASON

The Prince Regent's name does not appear in the list of Grand Master Masons given in the 1962 Year Book – the only Royal Grand Master shown there is HRH The Duke of York, later HM King George VI – although Laurie's *History of Freemasonry and the Grand Lodge of Scotland (1859)* shows that he was elected Grand Master and Patron of the Craft in Scotland on St Andrew's Day, 1805, and on each succeeding St Andrew's Day unitl 1819, the year before he ascended the throne as King George IV, Further search seemed desirable and this led to Murray Lyon's History. *History of the Lodge of Edinburgh (St Mary's Chapel) (1900).*

Murray Lyon records that HM King George III had seven sons who reached manhood and that six of these became freemasons. Their grandfather, Frederick Lewis, Prince of Wales, was the first undoubted admission to lodge membership of a Prince of the Blood Royal; he was entered in a lodge at the Palace of Kew in 1737, by Dr Desaguliers who had visited the Lodge of Edinburgh (Mary's Chapel) in 1721. Three of the six sons of King George III were the three Grand Masters in 1813. George, Prince of Wales and Prince Regent, the eldest son, was entered in 1787 at a special meeting of a Lodge in London presided over by his uncle, the Duke of Cumberland, who was Grand Master of the Grand Lodge of England (Moderns) at that time. The fourth son, Edward, Duke of Kent, father of Queen Victoria, joined Union Lodge in Geneva in 1789. The sixth son, Augustus, Duke of Susex, was initiated in Berlin in 1798.

When the Duke of Cumberland died in 1790 the Prince of Wales succeeded him as Grand Master of the Grand Lodge of England (Moderns), and continued as Grand Master until 1813 when he retired in favour of the Duke of Sussex, who became Grand Master of the United Grand Lodge of England in that year. The Duke of Sussex is said to have held several masonic meetings at Kensington Palace in which he was supported by brethren of the most exalted rank and that, on occasion, the famous Duke of Wellington acted as his Senior Warden. It is also recorded 'on good authority' that arrangements had been made by the Duke of Sussex for the initiation of the Prince

Consort but unfortunately the latter died before this could take place.

Murray Lyon did not include the name of George, Prince of Wales and Prince Regent in the list of Grand Master Masons in his History. In a Chapter (XLIII) dealing with the association of Royalty with masonry, he observes that prior to 1805 the Grand Lodge of Scotland had not aspired to the patronage of Royalty but on St Andrew's Day of that year HRH the Prince of Wales was elected Grand Master and Patron; that this was a title, and nothing more than a title, because the Prince was ineligible for election to the Grand Mastership not being a member of a Scottish lodge; that it was conferred upon him annually by Grand Lodge until his succession to the Crown in 1820 when the title was changed to that of Patron; that His Royal Highness never appeared in Grand Lodge although he visited Edinburgh in 1822, some two years after ascending the throne.

With all deference to a masonic historian of the standing of Murray Lyon I cannot help feeling that he was somewhat hard on this Royal Brother in playing down his Grand Mastership and (I make bold to claim) in failing to appreciate the significance of the part played by the Prince and the Earl of Moira, the Prince's able henchman and acting Grand Master for many years in England and for two years in Scotland, in first bringing together the Grand Lodge of England and Grand Lodge of Scotland and then bringing about the union of the two Grand Lodges in England. It seems to me, after reading through the Minutes of Grand Lodge from 1803 onwards, that the Prince's election as Grand Master Mason of Scotland in 1805 was the first stage in a carefully prepared plan designed to bring about the union of the two Grand Lodges in England, one of which (and that presumably not the right one) already had close ties with the Grand Lodge of Scotland, ties which dated from 1772 when the Duke of Athole, then Grand Master Elect of Scotland, became Grand Master of the Ancients. It was surely no mere coincidence that, in 1813, just before the union of the two Grand Lodges in England took place, the Prince should give up one of his Grand Masterships, namely that of the Grand Lodge of England which he had held for over twenty years, in favour of his brother, the Duke of Sussex while the Duke of Athole, who had been Grand Master of the Ancients for so long, should give up the Grand Mastership of the other Grand Lodge, in favour of another brother, the Duke of Kent. When the culminating point of union was reached in England, three Royal Brothers were the Grand Masters of the three Grand Lodges. The Duke of Kent then withdrew from the scene leaving the Duke of Sussex, a newcomer as Grand Master in England, to become the first Grand Master of the United Grand Lodge of England, the Prince remaining as Grand Master Mason of Scotland until his succession to the throne in 1820 prevented him from continuing other than as Patron.

In coming to the conclusion that the Prince of Wales and Prince Regent (later HM George IV) was not a 'pukka' Grand Master Mason of Scotland between 1805 and 1820, Murray Lyon seems to have been influenced by three main points – *firstly* that the election was invalid because the Prince was not a member of a Scottish Lodge; *secondly* that the title Grand Master Mason was merely conferred on him each year, and *thirdly*, that he never took his place in Grand Lodge.

On the first point, I find nothing in the *Laws and Regulations* of Grand Lodge in force at the time of his election in 1805, that required him to be a member of a Scottish lodge. According to these *Laws and Regulations* Grand Lodge consisted of a Grand Master, Grand Master Depute and Substitute and other office-bearers; the Master and Wardens of the Edinburgh lodges; and the Masters of Country lodges and their Wardens, or proxies and their wardens regularly appointed as representing lodges in the country. No brother could be a member of Grand Lodge unless he was a Master Mason. The Grand Master could choose his own Depute unless Grand Lodge chose a Grand Master Elect to succeed him; in that case the Grand Master Elect became the Grand Master Depute. Incidentally the first Grand Master Elect, chosen in 1760, was the Earl of Elgin and Kincardine, the present Grand Master Mason's great-great-great-grandfather. The only provision in the *Laws and Regulations* which might have affected the Prince, and that later, was one that the Grand Master must not serve for a longer period than two years successively. As present Chairman of the Laws and Rulings Committee I take the view that only Masters and Wardens of Edinburgh and Country Lodges had to be members of Scottish Lodges and that the Prince (as well as other directly elected office-bearers), was not debarred from becoming Head of the order in Scotland merely because he was not a member of a Scottish lodge. The Earl of Moira was elected Acting Grand Master Elect at the same time as the Prince was elected Grand Master Mason and his name was included in Murray Lyon's list as Grand Master from 1806 to 1808 but there is no evidence to show that *he* was a member of a Scottish lodge. Indeed everything points to his not having been a member. As regards the maximum period of two years in office, Grand Lodge simply did not apply this to the Grand Master Mason.

On the second point, I Think that the paragraphs which follow prove that the Prince and the Earl of Moira were well and truly elected members of Grand Lodge. On the third point, the Minutes of Grand Lodge bear out that it was not unusual for a Grand Master, or Acting Grand Master between 1805 and 1820, not to appear at a single meeting of Grand Lodge in his term of two years, which included two Grand Election meetings. It was not, of course, an easy matter for Grand Masters to come to Edinburgh for meetings and the Substitute Grand Master usually continued in office for many years and occupied the Chair at important meetings; often the Master of an Edinburgh lodge took the Chair.

What seems to have escaped Murray Lyon's notice was that the Prince's appointment as Grand Master Mason was part of a wider plan, a master plan of union of Scotland and England, probably formulated in England. The appointment of an Acting Grand Master followed the pattern of the Grand Lodge of England, that is, a Head of the Order (the same Royal Brother) with an Acting Grand Master under him elected to preside at meetings of Grand Lodge. How the master plan of union unfolded over the years, can be traced in Grand Lodge

Minutes which are easily followed in the fine handwriting of the period. Operations under the master plan began on St Andrew's Day, 30th November 1803. After the Grand Election the new Grand Master Elect, the Earl of Dalhousie (in the Grand Master's absence) led the brethren in procession from the New Church Aisle to the Tron Church where they listened to 'an appropriate and eloquent sermon' the text of which, taken from a passage in Hebrew, was 'Let Brotherly Love Continue'. At the Festival of St Andrew the chief guest was the Earl of Moira, Commander-in-Chief of the Forces in Scotland and Acting Grand Master of the Grand Lodge of England under the Prince of Wales. He made a stirring speech, in which he referred to the misunderstandings between the two English Grand Lodges and called for closer ties between the Grand Lodges of Scotland and England. Alex Laurie in his History which appeared in the following year, observed – 'From the presence of this Nobleman, the friends of the Grand Lodge of England anticipated an union between that respectable body and the Grand Lodge of Scotland.' His History closed on the following note:

> From this period we may date the origin of an union between the Grand Lodges of Scotland and that of England which we trust will soon be effected. From such a junction under the auspices of HRH the Prince of Wales, aided by the distinguished talents and respectability of the Earl of Moira and the abilities and conciliating manners of the Earl of Dalhousie, Free Masonry we hope will receive additional respectability and vigour and preserve in these Kingdoms its primitive purity and simplicity.

The next step was taken at the Quarterly Communication on 6 August 1804. Brother Alex Laurie (the historian and Assistant Grand Secretary at the time), moved, and this was duly seconded, 'That a communication be opened between the Grand Lodge of England under the auspices of HRH the Prince of Wales and the Grand Lodge of Scotland and that necessary measures be adopted that the same friendly intercourse should take place between these Grand Lodges as at present subsist between the Grand Lodge of Scotland and the

Grand Lodge of England under His Grace the Duke of Athole.'

Brother Laurie's motion was adopted on 5 November 1804, and a Committee was appointed to consider the steps to be taken to carry it into effect. The Committee recommended (this was confirmed at an adjourned Communication on 12 November) that the Earl of Dalhousie, who was to be the new Grand Master, should deliver in person a copy of the motion to the Earl of Moira. After the Grand Election on 30 November, the Earl of Dalhousie, now Grand Master, the Earl of Moira and some 1,500 brethren walked in procession from Parliament Hall to the Theatre Royal to celebrate St Andrew's Festival. During the toasts the Grand Master referred to the resolution he had been instructed to hand to the Earl of Moira and the latter 'replied in a speech of considerable length and ability and information in which he indicated that friendly intercourse would be opened with the other Grand Lodge.' On 5 August 1805, Grand Lodge had before them a resolution by the Grand Lodge of England, dated 10 April, reciprocating their wishes to be on terms of confidential communication, and in their turn Grand Lodge resolved '. . . it will be their study to promote and cherish that friendship and brotherly intercourse so happily begun . . .' They also appointed a Committee, headed by the Grand Master, to return grateful thanks to the Earl of Moira. At the Communication on 4 November 1805 coming events began to cast shadows. It was proposed, in his absence, that the Earl of Dalhousie, should be re-elected Grand Master but the choice of a Grand Master Elect had to be postponed because William, 17th Earl of Errol, declined to accept that office. At an adjourned communication on 18 November, arrangements for St Andrew's Festival were made; one of these was the charge, four shillings for speculative brethren and three shillings and sixpence for operative brethren. By the time of the second adjourned Communication, two days before St Andrew's Day, events had really begun to move. The Interim Substitute Grand Master, in the Chair, said that he had been with the Earl of Dalhousie and by his authorisation proposed the following as officers for the next year – HRH

George, Prince of Wales, Grand Master Mason and Patron of the Craft; The Rt Hon George, Earl of Dalhousie, acting Grand Master under His Royal Highness; The Rt Hon Francis, Earl of Moira, Commander-in-Chief for Scotland, Acting Grand Master Elect; The Rev Sir Henry Moncrieff Welwood, Bart, Grand Chaplain. This 'nomination was received with every demonstration of Masonic approbation and unanimously agreed to.'

St Andrew's Day on 2 December 1805, must have been an historic one. The minutes record that at the Grand Election, after the roll call and after the names of members had been taken down, the Interim Substitute Grand Master rose and congratulated the brethren at large and the Grand Lodge in particular on the return of their anniversary and in order that the brethren might have it again in their power to exercise the right of election so generously and patriotically bestowed upon them by St Clair of Roslin, he declared all offices vacant and left the Chair. Upon this the Earl of Aboyne, Past Grand Master, immediately proposed HRH George, Prince of Wales to be Grand Master Mason and Patron of the Craft in Scotland. 'This nomination met with most unbounded applause and universal Masonic approbation.' Thereafter the Earl of Aboyne proposed the Rt Hon George, Earl of Dalhousie to be Acting Grand Master under His Royal Highness. This nomination was likewise universally approved, whereupon the Earl was introduced by the two Grand Wardens, sworn into office, clothed and invested with the proper insignia. The Earl 'returned his sincere thanks for this additional mark of distinction particularly to preside over the Masons of Scotland as Acting Grand Master under so illustrious a Personage as His Royal Highness the Prince of Wales.' The Earl of Dalhousie then proposed his Excellency the Earl of Moira, Commander-in-Chief of HM Forces in Scotland, to be Acting Grand Master Elect, which met with unanimous approbation and his Lordship having been introduced in due form, was clothed and sworn into office. After the Grand Election, the Grand Lodge and brethren walked in procession by torchlight from Parliament Hall to the Kings Arms Tavern to celebrate the Festival of St Andrew. 'Owing to the great number of Brethren who attended the procession and were anxious to get into the Great Hall a considerable degree of confusion was occasioned and continued for some time but this having at last subsided, order and regularity was maintained throughout the remainder of the evening. Many Masonic, Loyal and Patriotic toasts were drunk.'

At the Grand Election on 1 December 1806, His Royal Highness was 'with unbounded approbation and applause re-elected as Grand Master Mason and Patron of the Craft and the Earl of Moira was elected Acting Grand Master under his Royal Highness.' The Earl of Moira was not present on this occasion (nor did he attend the following year) and there was no festival because of the General Election which made it difficult for members to attend and for the military to line the route, hold the torches, etc. On 3 August 1807, a Charter was granted to brethren in Andalusia in Spain for a lodge to be called 'The Desired Re-union'.

During the fourteen years in which the Prince of Wales was Grand Master Mason and Patron, the procedure at Grand Elections followed much the same pattern as in 1805. The brother in the Chair (usually Brother William Inglis of Middleton, who became Substitute Grand Master in 1805) congratulated the brethren at large and the Grand Lodge in particular on the return of the anniversary and reminded the brethren of the power and privilege vested in them, of electing their office-bearers. The principal office-bearers were then elected. Those usually named in the Minutes were (1) the Grand Master Mason and Patron of the Craft (HRH the Prince of Wales was unanimously elected each year from 1805 to 1819), (2) the 'Acting Grand Master under His Royal Highness', and (3) the Acting Grand Master Elect (at the beginning of the Acting Grand Master's second term). Grand Lodge Minutes clearly show that throughout the years the Prince was Grand Master Mason, no brother was called, or used the title of, Grand Master or Grand Master Elect. It was always Acting Grand Master, or Acting Grand Master under His Royal Highness, and Acting Grand Master Elect. This certainly does not suggest that Grand Lodge considered 'Grand Master Mason' to be a nominal title. The choice of the title was probably a revival of that of St Clair of Roslin although Laurie's History contains a copy of one letter (there are few letters in the History) dated 9 June 1800, to HM George III (following a recent attempt on his life) in which the Grand Master, Sir James Stirling, Lord Provost of Edinburgh, signed his name over the title 'Grand Master Mason of Scotland'. In a general chapter of his History (Chap. IV), Laurie records that on resigning his Hereditary Grand Mastership on the formation of Grand Lodge in 1736, St Clair was on St Andrew's Day of that Year, 'elected as Grand Master and proclaimed as Grand Master Mason of all Scotland'. The title Grand Master Mason also probably enabled the brother who would otherwise have been Grand Master to carry those two words in his title, 'Acting Grand Master' (as in the Grand Lodge of England), without impinging on the title of the Head of the Order. Laurie also records in his History that Grand Lodge had already made a decision on the importance of the title of the Head of the Order. He states that on 7 August 1786, Grand Lodge ordained 'that the Brethren in all time coming shall address no Master by the style or title of *Grand* but he who shall have the honour to be chosen *Grand Master of Scotland* that title belonging to *none* but *him* so chosen'.

At the Grand Election on 30 November 1820, the first after the Prince ascended the throne, Grand Lodge did not revert to the pre-1805 title of Grand Master. The Substitute Grand Master, after declaring the offices vacant proposed HM King George the Fourth be continued Grand Patron of the Ancient Order of St John's Masonry of Scotland and His Grace Alexander, Duke of Hamilton and Brandon be Grand Master Mason of Scotland. From this year onwards the title Grand Master Mason first used regularly for the Prince, seems to have come into general use instead of Grand Master.

The introductory remarks from the Chair at Grand Elections reminding the brethren of their right to elect whom they chose, the unanimous election of the Prince each year, the election each year of a brother to act under him as Acting Grand Master (the same title as in England), and the attitude of Grand Lodge generally, in my humble opinion, prove conclusively that over the years 1805 to 1819, Grand Lodge definitely chose and regarded the Prince of Wales and Prince Regent, later HM George IV, as Grand Master Mason of Scotland. Apart from these facts, Grand Lodge as a sovereign body solemnly and deliberately making the same decision year after year must surely be held to have overcome any Constitutional bar if there ever was one.

The perhaps more important union, that of the two Grand Lodges in England, took place on St John's Day, 27 December 1813. At an Extraordinary meeting of The Grand Lodge of Scotland, on 20 December 1813, a number of documents were before Grand Lodge, including a joint letter, dated 7 December, from the Dukes of Kent and Sussex addressed to the Acting Grand Master, Lord Viscount Duncan. Unfortunately, a space for this letter in the minutes has been left blank. There are, however, in copper-plate handwriting, copies of other documents, including a letter from the Grand Lodge of England under the Old Institutions (the last letter from the Ancients), written 'in command from their Royal Highnesses the Dukes of Kent and Sussex', transmitting Articles of Union agreed upon by the two Grand Masters which had been solemnly ratified, sealed and exchanged by both Grand Lodges. The letter also included the following invitation – 'You will perceive by Art. IV (of the Articles of Union) it is proposed for the great purpose of establishing perfect uniformity and binding the whole Masonic world in one brotherhood on the day of Union to solicit the presence of one or two enlightened brethren of the Grand Lodges of Ireland and Scotland.' Among the documents enclosed were copies of proceedings of the Grand Lodge of Ancients showing that the Duke of Kent had become Grand Master. At an Especial Grand Lodge on 8 November 1813, the Duke of Athole having intimated his desire to resign in favour of the Duke of Kent, the latter was elected as Grand Master. At another Especial Grand Lodge on 1 December 1813, the Duke of

Sussex and others of his Grand Officers, having in the meantime been made Ancient Masons, saw the Duke of Kent installed and proclaimed as Grand Master under the Old Institutions.

With the union of the two Grand Lodges in England on 27 December 1813 and the Prince Regent's succession to the throne in 1820, the chief characters in this exercise in history fade away. The name of The Earl of Dalhousie appeared again some sixty-five years after the 9th Earl proposed George, Prince of Wales, as Grand Master Mason, in connection with the association of another Prince of Wales with the Scottish Craft. Murray Lyon states that it was the 11th Earl of Dalhousie, Grand Master at the time, who proposed that HRH Albert Edward, Prince of Wales (later HM Edward VII) should become Patron of the Order in Scotland; he installed him in that office in October 1870.

The brother who made the most profound personal impact on Grand Lodge was perhaps the Earl of Moira, the power behind the masonic thrones. Although he did not appear in Grand Lodge during his two years as Acting Grand Master he kept in touch and gave his and the Prince's views on important topics. Two of his speeches have already been referred to, those on St Andrew's days 1803 and 1804, but he seems to have excelled himself on 21 November 1809, at the consecration of the first Freemasons' Hall (St Cecilia's Hall). As Past Acting Grand Master he presided on that occasion and the Minutes say of him – 'In a speech of the greatest eloquence and most transcendent ability gave a luminous exordium upon Masonry, the Force of which was felt by every individual in the Hall but which it is impossible here to do justice in any attempt at recapitulation.' Laurie says in his History,

> The dedication of this Temple to Masonry (the first Freemasons' Hall) by so distinguished a Craftsman may be said to have closed the brilliant Masonic career of his Lordship in Scotland; and it was with unfeigned regret that the Scottish Craft beheld the departure from among them of this highly esteemed Brother – who besides his other distinctions had enjoyed the rare felicity of being Acting Grand Master of the Grand Lodges both of England and Scotland

during the same period. Shortly afterwards he was appointed, under the title of Marquess of Hastings, Governor General and Commander-in-Chief in India, a sphere well suited to his talents both as a statesman and a soldier and where from his mild and benignant sway he became the idol of all classes in that vast portion of the British Empire.

13

OUR RITUAL
A Study in its Development

J. Mason Allan

IT MAY COME as a surprise to many brethren to learn that our Craft Ritual, in the form in which we know it today, does not date farther back than 1835 or thereabouts. That does not mean, of course, that the elements of which it is composed or at least most of them, do not go back very far indeed, but it does mean that we have no evidence that these elements were combined before that date into the 'peculiar system of morality veiled in allegory and illustrated by symbol' with which we are familiar today. It will be our present purpose to pass under review some early masonic records and from them establish historical facts on which the foregoing conclusion is based, and at the same time to present some other considerations that may have a bearing upon the development of our ritual.

Most craftsmen believe, and believe correctly, that the freemasonry of today is, in a very real sense, the lineal descendant of the old Masons' Gild. In the Middle Ages many trades had their Gilds, but the Masons' Gild differed from all the others in two very important respects. In the first place, most tradesmen carried on their vocations in fixed localities where they were all well known to one another and to their employers. But the masons, because of the nature of their work were necessarily mobile – settled for a time while engaged on the building of (say) a Cathedral or a Royal Palace, and when their work there was completed travelling, sometimes a considerable distance, to the site of the next building on which they would be employed. They were not so well known to one another or to employers of labour, and when one professing to be a mason presented himself at a building site seeking employment, it was necessary for the employer not only to prove, by a practical test, that the man was capable of skilled work, but also to be satisfied that he had been regularly received into the Gild, a necessary condition of employment in those days. Hence the need for such 'test' questions as we find in the catechism part of the *Edinburgh Register House* MS (1696): 'Some Questions that Masons used to put to those who have the Word before they will acknowledge them.'

In the second place, the masons alone had 'charges' that were addressed to apprentices when they were indentured to their masters. These are commonly spoken of as *The Old Charges*. The two oldest that have been preserved are *The Regius Poem* (it is written in rhyme) believed to date from 1390, and the *Cooke MS.* about 1425. Another in the possession of the Grand Lodge of England is dated 1583, and some others were written in the seventeenth century. Brothers Pick and Knight, in their *Pocket History of Freemasonry* say: 'Although parallels may be found here and there, no other medieval body, whether craft, religious or otherwise, is known to have possessed such documents.' They also say: 'It is remarkable that Scotland produced no traditional history such as England had from about 1400 in the Old Charges. The few copies associated with Scotland are obviously copied from England, indeed one or two naïvely require the Craftsman to be true to the King of England.'

A short description of elements that are common to all or most of these Old Charges will be of interest and are relevant to our present purpose. They all open with a prayer which, as is to be expected at that period, is definitely Christian in character, including an invocation of the Holy Trinity. Then follows a 'traditional history' of the Craft, which is in many respects fantastic, but which contains some elements that are not unfamiliar to us today. They deal with the seven liberal Arts and Sciences – Grammar, Rhetoric, Logic, Arithmetic,

Geometry, Music and Astronomy. These Arts and Sciences were written on two pillars of stone – 'the one stone was called marble, that cannot burn with fire. The other was called Lateral (*ie*, brick or tile) that cannot drown with water'. That detail, with a slight modification and transposition, will be familiar to many. And there are some students who believe that we have here the original legend of 'Two Pillars', a later version of which finds embodiment in other Pillars that are alluded to in the *Edinburgh Register House* MS., in all the eighteenth-century catechisms, and in our present-day rituals.

At this point several versions of the Old Charges require the Apprentice to take an OB on the VSL. Then follow the 'general' Charges, which relate not only to the craft and its secrets, but also to general conduct. The Apprentice is charged:

1. To be true to God and Holy Church;
2. To be a true liegeman to the King and his Council;
3. To be true to one another, and to do to others as he would that others should do to him;
4. To keep the secrets of the craft;
5. Not to be a thief;
6. To be loyal to his master and to serve him for his profit and advantage;
7. To call masons fellows or brothers and no foul name, not to take a fellows' wife violently, nor his daughter ungodly, nor his servant in villany;
8. To pay his way honestly, wherever he may go; and
9. To do no villany in any house where he may be entertained.

Then follow some particular Charges for Masters and Fellows; but these relate entirely to the operative work of the craft.

These details are given here for three reasons: (1) because in them we can recognise much that is in the ethical instruction given in our modern ritual; (2) because the method of giving such a 'charge' is continued in the Charges that are given today at the conclusion of the ceremonies of Entering, Passing and Raising and also in the Charges read to the Master of a Lodge at his installation; and (3) because failure to read these Old

Charges was one of the allegations brought by the Antients against the Moderns which will be dealt with later.

Thus it can be clearly seen that any study of the development of our Ritual must begin with the Old Charges and their contents.

In the days when masons followed the work from building site to building site, a 'lodge' would be formed at each site. This was probably discontinued gradually as the erection of Great buildings such as cathedrals, palaces or castles grew less and masons became more settled in towns where they were employed in more ordinary building. Then they formed what Brother Douglas Knoop calls 'territorial lodges'. The *Schaw Statutes* (1599) make mention of lodges at Edinburgh, Kilwinning and Stirling – and these three lodges are still actively working, Knoop and Jones, in *The Genesis of Freemasonry* (page 52) state that 'the only independent evidence of the ownership, or the use, of versions of the MS, *Constitutions*' (*ie*, the Old Charges) 'by operative masons relates to lodges at Stirling, Melrose, Kilwinning, Aberdeen, Dumfries, Aitcheson's Haven, Alnwick and Swallwell'. Six of these eight lodges were in Scotland; but it is interesting to note that the lodge of Edinburgh is not included. The other two lodges were in Northumberland, and both had a very close linkage, masonically, with Scotland. (See *The Genesis of Freemasonry*, pages 221 and 222). This list is given here to establish two points: (1) that lodges at that time were localised or 'territorial', and (2) that the Old Charges continued to be used after the Lodges were so localised. Pick and Knight in their *Pocket History* state that in England 'the operative Lodge is almost unknown' – (presumably they mean in a 'territorial' sense). When Elias Ashmole was admitted to the lodge at Warrington in 1646, none but non-operative masons were present.

It was no doubt after the settling of lodges at fixed centres that non-operative members began to be admitted. The earliest record of a non-operative being present at a meeting of an operative lodge is to be found in the minutes of the Lodge of Edinburgh for 8 June 1600, which were attested by all present, including James Boswell of Auchenleck, an ancestor of the biographer of Dr Johnson. Three others were admitted to the same lodge in 1634 – twelve years before the admission of Elias Ashmole to the lodge at Warrington.

The seventeenth century may be regarded as the period when the transition from operative to speculative got well under way. Influence in that direction no doubt came from men like Ashmole and Sir Robert Moray, one of the Founders of the Royal Society (who was admitted by the lodge of Edinburgh at a meeting in Newcastle on 20 May 1641), and possibly, indirectly, from others of similar interests. Space does not permit of enlarging upon this matter; but one brief quotation (which may later be found to have considerable relevance to our present study) may be given from a well-known masonic historian, Robert Freke Gould. In his *History of Freemasonry* (Vol II, page 138) he expresses the opinion that 'during the sixteenth and seventeenth centuries, Kabalism and Rosicrucianism profoundly influenced many secret societies in Europe; and Freemasonry received no slight tinge from the Kabalistic pursuits of some of its adherents at that time'. Brother Gould, a doughty champion of the principles of the 'Authentic School' of masonic historians, was exceedingly cautious and careful in his scrutiny of evidence, and we may take it that he would not have ventured to make such a categorical statement unless he was satisfied that it was fully justified by the cumulative effect of all the available evidence – no doubt in great measure 'circumstantial'. Such a statement by such a man is worthy of the most serious consideration.

He is certainly supported in his statement by a still more learned student of masonic and cognate matters, who, however, approaches the subject from a somewhat different angle, Brother A. E. Waite, who says: 'It seems to me quite certain that Kabalism has transmitted elements to our secret societies, and it is not less certain that the men who elaborated our (Masonic) rituals had some personal knowledge of the secret doctrine of the Kabalah.' He was, of course, referring to our modern rituals.

Towards the end of the seventeenth century we come to the

Edinburgh Register House MS., which is the first of a series of catechisms which continued to appear until well into the eighteenth century. Three of these – the *Edinburgh Register House* MS (1696), the *Graham* MS (1726), and *Masonry Dissected* (1730) were dealt with in detail in an article on 'The Five Points of Fellowship' in the Grand Lodge of Scotland Year Book for 1959. Here it is proposed only to pick out one or two points that are relevant to our immediate purpose.

These catechisms are not ritual as we now understand that word. They consist of questions and answers which, however, refer back in specific terms to some ceremony that had taken place previously. Of these ceremonies themselves we know nothing except what may be inferred from the questions and answers. They were probably very short and simple, restricted to the formal introduction of new Apprentices and Fellows, and the communication of the Word and other Secrets. That there was possibly no set form for this may be gathered from the narrative portion of the *Edinburgh Register House* MS. There we read: 'Then all the masons present whisper among themselves the word, beginning with the youngest, until it come to the master mason, who gives the word to the entered Apprentice.' In this short quotation there are two expressions that call for comment as relevant to our present purpose: 'the word' and 'entered apprentice'.

The earliest known reference to the Mason Word is in The Muses' Threnodie, a metrical account of Perth and neighbourhood by Henry Adamson, published in Edinburgh in 1638, which contains these lines:

> 'For we be brethren of the *Rosie Crosse*,
> We have the Mason Word and second sight.'

Brother Douglas Knoop, in *The Genesis of Freemasonry* (page 222) says that 'there is no evidence to show that the Mason Word was ever used among English operative masons except possibly in the North'. These last words would cover such lodges as those at Alnwick and Swallwell already mentioned. He also says that 'various entries in Lodge records in the seventeenth and eighteenth centuries refer to the Mason

Word; those records, without exception, refer to Scottish Lodges'. And, finally, he says: 'The purpose of the Mason Word was to distinguish masons who were members of their trade organisation from others who were not. The need for some secret method of recognition arose from two conditions peculiar to Scotland, *viz.*, the possibility of employment open to cowans, and the existence of an industrial grade without exact parallel in England, that of entered apprentice.' Apprentices who were bound to their masters by indenture did not require any special mode of recognition. But when they had completed their indentured service, they became 'entered' apprentices – journeymen they would be called today. The expression entered apprentices was not known in England until the publication of the first *Book of Constitution* in 1723, which was compiled by Rev James Anderson, DD – a Scotsman!

In passing, it may be remaked that 'Fellow of Craft' is also distinctively Scottish. It appears in the *Schaw Statutes* (1599), but in England it was not known until 1723; and there it is generally used without the 'of' – *ie*, 'Fellow Craft'.

Let us now revert to the *Graham* MS (1726) which is of special importance for a study of the development of our Ritual. This MS makes very clear reference to King Solomon and Hiram Abiff, and their respective parts in the building of the Temple:

> Four hundred and four score years after the Children of Israel came out of the land of Egypt, in the fourth year of Solomon's reign over Israel, that Solomon began to build the House of the Lord. . . . Now we read in the 13th verse of the 7th chapter of the First Book of Kings that Solomon sent and fetched Hiram out of Tyre, he being a widow's son of the Tribe of Naphtali, and his father was a man of Tyre, a worker in brass. . . . And he came to King Solomon and wrought all his work for him.

This is very familiar to us. But the MS does not go on to give us the legend of our Third Degree which has Hiram as its central figure. Instead, it does give practically all the ingredients of that legend in a very different setting, with a traditional history of which Noah was the central figure – which may be taken as about 1,300 years before the building of King Solomon's Temple.

By the death of Noah some secret knowledge was lost. His three sons, Shem, Ham and Japheth, went to their father's grave 'to try if they could find anything about him to lead them to the vertuable secrets which this famous preacher had.' But before they went they 'had already agreed that if they did not find the very thing itself, the first thing they found was to be to them as a secret . . .' There we have the earliest reference to substituted secrets.

When they came to the grave they found 'nothing but the dead body almost consumed away'. Because of its condition their first efforts to raise it failed. But ultimately 'they raised up the dead body, setting foot to foot, knee to knee, breast to breast, cheek to cheek, and hand to back'. In this old Noah legend the MS gives several other details that are almost identical with elements in our Hiramic Legend. And also, incidentally, it contains some dramatic details with which our modern Mark Degree has made us familiar.

The first record of the Hiramic Legend appears in Samuel Pritchard's *Masonry Dissected* which was published in 1730 – four years after the date of the *Graham* MS. The appearance, at dates so close to one another, of two legends so similar in content but so vastly different in setting and in the periods to which they are assigned by their respective 'traditional histories', is very striking indeed. In this connection Brothers Pick and Knight, in their *Pocket History of Freemasonry* say: 'It is probable that, before the Craft finally settled on the building of King Solomon's Temple, and the loss and recovery of certain Knowledge, other prototypes were tried out, perhaps by small groups of Masons in isolated parts of the country.' We may agree, broadly, with what is implied in this conjecture; but it raises two very interesting questions: (1) *who*, at this period, constituted 'the Craft' which ultimately decided in favour of the Hiramic version – or, more briefly, *who* made the decision; and (2) did they come to their decision deliberately after a consideration of the experiments made with various prototypes? We shall have occasion to revert to these questions at a later stage.

In 1717 the first Grand Lodge of England had been formed.

Its jurisdiction was at first confined to London and Westminster, but it gradually spread throughout England, where many lodges had long been functioning. There had also been many lodges actively operating in Ireland and Scotland. The Grand Lodge of Ireland was formed in 1725 and the Grand Lodge of Scotland in 1736. These simple historical facts are stated to introduce the next phase of our study in the development of our Ritual.

According to Bernard Jones in the *Freemason's Guide and Compendium* Freemasons from Ireland and Scotland 'were drifting into England and bringing with them ideas which had grown up not on English soil, but which, nevertheless, were very precious to those who held them. Grand Lodge was probably very worried, somewhere about 1730, at the number of unaffiliated masons coming apparently from nowhere and claiming admission to their lodges.' In order to make admission of such men to lodges more difficult, Grand Lodge issued an order to make certain changes in the methods of 'proving' or testing, including the transportation of the words of the First and Second Degrees; but not all lodges obeyed this order. Many lodges in England had an appreciable proportion of members of Irish origin, and no doubt many Scottish Masons also had migrated to England; and the influence of these would tend towards the maintenance of the older tradition and practice. In any case, the lodges that were in opposition to Grand Lodge on this or other grounds – most of which had never come under the jurisdiction of Grand Lodge – gradually grew together, and probably as early as 1739 a Committee had been formed to co-ordinate their activities, and the work of that Committee culminated in the formation of a rival Grand Lodge in 1751. Then ensued a long period of bitter rivalry between the two Grand Lodges until their union in 1813. The history of this period is not only intrinsically interesting to masonic students, but it also provides much material that is relevant to our present study.

The new Grand Lodge took the title of 'The Most Antient and Honourable Society of Free and Accepted Masons'. They claimed that they had adhered to the Antient Landmarks of the

Order, from which the others had departed, and on this account they became known as the Antients, while the older Grand Lodge were dubbed the Moderns; and both these designations have been retained ever since.

Among the defections of which the Antients accused the Moderns, the following may be noted as relevant to our present purpose:
1. That they had ceased to read the Old Charges at initiations, thus abandoning a Landmark.
2. That they had de-Christianised Freemasonry. The Old Charges had been, almost without exception, of a positively Christian character; but the first of the Regulations that were embodied in Anderson's *Constitutions* of 1723 stated that "tis now thought more expedient only to oblige them (*ie*, the Freemasons) to that Religion to which all men agree, leaving their particular opinions to themselves'.
3. That they had transposed the modes of recognition of the First and Second Degrees – as already indicated above.
4. That they omitted the Deacons from their Office-bearers.
5. That they had abandoned the esoteric ceremony of Installed Master.
6. That they had curtailed the ceremonies, and in particular had neglected the 'Lectures', or catechisms, attached to each Degree.

The Grand Lodges of Ireland and Scotland had sympathised with those lodges who had resisted the changes ordered by the original Grand Lodge, and they maintained very close and amicable relations with the new Grand Lodge when it was formed in 1751. It may be of interest to note how close that relationship was at the highest levels. In 1756 a former Grand Master of Ireland, the Earl of Blessington, was elected Grand Master of the Antients. He was succeeded, in 1760, by the Earl of Kellie, who was Grand Master Mason of Scotland in 1763-65. The third Duke of Atholl was Grand Master of the Antients from 1771 to 1774 and Grand Master Mason of Scotland in 1773, so that he held both offices simultaneously for a period. The same is true of the fourth Duke of Atholl, who was Grand Master Mason of Scotland 1778–1779 and was Grand Master of the Antients from 1774 till 1781 and again from 1791 till 1813. And in the period between 1781 and 1791 the Grand Master of the Antients was the Marquis of Antrim, who was Grand Master of Ireland in 1773 and again in 1779. It may be of particular interest to Scottish Masons to know that the Antients were known as Atholl Masons, and even the official Year Book of the United Grand Lodge of England refers to the Atholl or Antient Grand Lodge. In 1813 the Duke of Atholl was succeeded by HRH the Duke of Kent, son of George III.

Though the rivalry between the two Grand Lodges in England was very acute, there were enlightened brethren in both bodies who realised the wrongness of this division and worked to find a way towards union. Ultimately, on 26 October 1809, the Modern Grand Lodge issued a Charter or Warrant to the Lodge of Promulgation, so named because it was formed 'for the purpose of promulgating the ancient Land Marks of the Society, and instructing the Craft in all matters and forms as may be necessary to be known by them . . .' The work done by this lodge represents the beginning of a process that culminated, nearly forty years later, in the final formulation of our modern ritual as we know it today.

The Lodge of Promulgation, when they had completed the work allotted to them, reported back to the Moderns Grand Lodge that they had 'a confident persuasion of having derived the most authentic information from the purest sources . . . as henceforth to render all the Ceremonies of the Craft, in practice simple, in effect impressive, and in all respects comfortable to ancient practice'. What this amounted to in actual fact was that they accepted practically all the Antient practices in matters on which there had been differences between the two bodies with one notable exception, namely, that they tacitly accepted the position reflected in the first Article in the Regulations incorporated in *Anderson's Constitutions* of 1723, referred to above. The Lodge of Promulgation ceased to function in 1811.

On the side of the Antients, their Grand Lodge appointed a

Committee in 1810 to explore the prospects of achieving union, and their report led to that Grand Lodge deciding 'that a Masonic Union, on principles equal and honourable to both Grand Lodges, and preserving the Land Marks of the Antient Craft would, in the opinion of this Grand Lodge, be expedient and advantageous to both'.

The union of the two Grand Lodges was finally effected and ratified on 1 December 1813. At that time the Duke of Sussex was Grand Master of the Moderns and the Duke of Kent Grand Master of the Antients. They were both brothers of the Prince Regent, afterwards King George IV. On the motion of HRH the Duke of Kent, HRH the Duke of Sussex was elected Grand Master of the United Grand Lodge, and he was installed as such on St John the Evangelist's Day, 27 December 1813, and he continued to hold that office for thirty years.

On 7 December 1813, six days after the Union had been ratified, the Lodge of Reconciliation was warranted. This Lodge was composed of well-known brethren from each Grand Lodge and its purpose was to reconcile the working of previous Modern Lodges and previous Antient Lodges so as to ensure uniformity of working in all the lodges throughout England. They built on the foundation that had been laid by the Lodge of Promulgation, and their method of procedure was to give demonstrations at various centres which the Masters of Lodges were invited to attend. They continued to function till 1816 and held twenty-six meetings. There are detailed records of twenty meetings, and from these records, considered in the light of subsequent history, and even though the Minutes make no reference to Lectures, it can be gathered that their demonstrations were not so much the actual working of the Degrees as a detailed description of the working given in the form of questions asked by the Master for the evening and answered by the Wardens for the evening – different brethren occupied these chairs at each meeting. At nine of the twenty meetings referred to above the Master's chair was occupied by the Rev Samuel Hemming, DD, who later compiled the famous 'Hemming Lectures' to which further reference will be made shortly. After the Lodge of Reconciliation ceased to function in 1816 their work was continued by Lodges of Instruction, of which the most famous were the Stability Lodge of Instruction, formed in 1817, and the Emulation Lodge of Improvement, formed in 1823.

It will be relevant to our present purpose to give more details regarding this method of giving instruction by means of the Lectures. This method corresponds exactly to the eighteenth-century Catechisms which embody references back to previous ceremonies, of which we otherwise know nothing, but of the nature of which we can gather something from the questions and answers. Similarly the early nineteenth-century Lectures refer back to the ceremonies of the three degrees; and it may be assumed with confidence that as the Lectures were developed by the Lodge of Reconciliation, the actual ceremonies were being developed *pari passu* and gradually took more definite form. By 1816 Brother Hemming had compiled Lectures on all three degrees, and these comprised 256 questions and answers on the First Degree, 145 on the Second Degree and 78 on the Third Degree. Ten years later a Minute of the Stability Lodge of Instruction, dated 21 April 1826, reads as follows: – 'The Rev Dr Hemming was invited to preside, when the Lecture (First Degree) was ably worked by the Rev Dr Samuel Hemming assisted by . . .' At the close, the grateful thanks of the Lodge were tendered to Brother Hemming for presiding and 'for the advantage they enjoy in the possession of that Lecture which he has arranged with such skill and talent as to stand unparalleled in the Masonic World'. According to the minutes, also, the Lodge seems to have worked only the Lecture on the First Degree until 28 September 1827, when that on the Second Degree is mentioned for the first time; and that on the Third Degree is not mentioned until 7 November 1828.

As already indicated, the Emulation Lodge of Improvement was not formed until six years after the Stability Lodge of Instruction. Brother C. D. Rotch, in his short treatise on *The Lodge of Reconciliation 1813–1816, and its Influence on Present-Day Ritual*, says: 'It is not easy to understand why the Stability and Emulation Lodges of Improvement preferred to work by Lectures only until after 1830.' This may be difficult to understand, but we must accept the fact, noting that it applies to Emulation as well as to Stability.

In the early days of the Emulation Lodge of Improvement the dominating figure was Brother Peter Gilkes, who, however, did not join it until two years after its formation. Brother Gilkes was a very significant personality in English Masonic history of this period. Regarding him, Brother Hiram Hallett in his short history of *The Lodges of Promulgation, Reconciliation, Stability and Emulation*, says: 'The Emulation Lodge of Improvement bases all its claims for pre-eminence on the assumption that they derive their Ritual from this famous masonic instructor.'

It may be relevant to give the following further quotation from Brother Hallett: 'When the method of imparting masonic Instruction by means of Lectures began it is impossible to say. About 1763 Lectures by William Hutchinson were published, and in 1772 William Preston published his version. The ceremonies in those days were short and simple; the Lectures were long and verbose . . . these Lectures, however, containing all the essentials of the three degrees. It is not now possible to state when the rehearsals of the ceremonies supplanted them.' The words 'long and verbose' are no doubt true of Hutchinson and Preston, but are scarcely so applicable to the eighteenth-century Catechisms or the nineteenth-century 'Lectures'.

The *Emulation Ritual* (known as the *Perfect Ceremonies of Craft Freemasonry*) was first published by 'A. Lewis' in 1838, but it may be taken for granted that MS copies were in circulation for some time before that. It may also be taken for granted that the *Stability Ritual* had been completed about the same time. Brother Rotch states that all the present-day rituals, except those of Ireland, Scotland and Bristol, may be said to be derived from Stability and Emulation. As regards the Scottish rituals, all those known to the present writer, with one notable exception in the West of Scotland, show extensive evidence of the influence of Emulation. For example, in the ceremony of opening the lodge, many Scottish lodges reproduce questions and answers in the Second Section of the First Degree Lecture; others retain the substance of these but alter the wording; and some introduce questions that are not in the *Emulation Ritual* but the substance of which is in the *Emulation Lectures*. Throughout the ceremonies – even in those lodges where the Third Degree is most 'dramatised' – there are many passages in which the language of Emulation is exactly or approximately reproduced. In the Obligations the language is very similar to Emulation, though in some rituals additional details are introduced. And even in the notable exception referred to above, there are several phrases that are characteristic of Emulation. These details are given here in support of the view that, notwithstanding the variety of workings in Scotland, there is at least a hard core in them all that is clearly the result of the development which it has been our purpose to outline in this paper.

The time has come to summarise the result of our study so far, and to point to some conclusions that may be drawn therefrom. We have seen that the first complete ritual was published in 1838. Before that, instruction was imparted by means of Lectures in the form of question and answer, and, in the Stability and Emulation Lodges at least, by that means only until 1830 or thereabouts. It may be inferred, therefore, that the ritual probably received its final form between those dates – say about 1835. The ritual of 1835, whether Stability, Emulation, or other, is, in respect of scope, structure and Landmarks, essentially the same as our present-day rituals, notwithstanding the wide variety of workings that characterise Scottish freemasonry. In these respects of scope, structure and Landmarks, it may be taken that all our Scottish Rituals derive ultimately from the 1835 ritual, though in other respects many of them contain features that are indigenous to and characteristic of Scotland. Conversely there are features in the 1835 ritual that had their original sources in Scotland.

We have also seen that in all our present-day rituals there are elements that are to be found in very early masonic MSS and other writings. Among these are the words B. and J. which we find in the *Edinburgh Register House* MS and in practically every eighteenth century Catechism. We must also include here the Hiramic Legend, which first appears in *Masonry Dissected* in 1730, but which appears to have been decided upon after a 'try-out' of the same theme in a very different setting in the Noah legend as set forth in the *Graham* MS (1726). But while the Noah legend was rejected for this purpose, there are many other elements in the *Graham* MS, including the idea of substituted secrets, that still characterise present-day masonry. And a perusal of other eighteenth-century Catechisms will reveal quite a number of significant details with which we are all familiar.

But there is also much in the 1835 ritual that was entirely new. To take but one example – the definition of freemasonry as 'A peculiar system of morality, veiled in allegory and illustrated by symbol' appears in the First Section of the First Degree Lecture – for the first time so far as the present writer is aware. And many other similar examples could be given. But by far the most significant, and entirely new, feature of the 1835 Ritual, was the wonderful way in which all the material that had accumulated during the seventeenth and eighteenth centuries had been examined, and elements therefrom selectively chosen with insight and discrimination, and built up into a peculiar system that is simply amazing in its symmetry, self-consistency and completeness. The men who could compile such a system were truly learned and expert brethren. Let us consider what evidence we can find in any modern ritual that they were truly learned and expert.

1. They obviously had an intimate knowledge of the Hebrew Scriptures; but
2. in the Hiramic Legend they departed, on a very essential point, from the Scriptural record in order to bring the legend into line with the central mythos of the Ancient Mystery cults – such as those of Osiris, Dionysus and others – in which the neophyte is identified with the tutelary hero. So it can be inferred that they had an intimate knowledge of these Ancient Mysteries.
3. It can also be assumed (though this is not explicitly indicated in the Legend itself, but may be inferred from

other intimations in the Ritual and from various allusions in the eighteenth-century Catechisms) that they were familiar with the supreme presentation of the same theme in the identification of the Christian neophyte with Christ in His death and resurrection.
4. They were certainly deeply versed in the Hebrew Kaballah, though this can only be recognised by those who are conversant with the Kaballah. But it may be stated that points that can more reasonably be attributed to Kaballistic origin than to any other source are – the three Pillars on which a Lodge of Freemasons figuratively rests; the Path of the Candidate, in the course of his initiations, between two Pillars, one on the left and the other on the right; and, above all, the point from which a MM cannot err, which the present writer regards as the most significant symbol in freemasonry with the exception of the TGL. If the Kaballistic association be adopted tentatively as a working hypothesis, a craftsman versed in the Kaballah would soon recognise not only that the whole framework of our system is Kaballistic, but also that a great many details that otherwise appear to have little or no particular point, acquire a very real significance.
5. A comparison of the TGL as a composite symbol with corresponding symbols in other systems will suggest that these learned brethren had an intimate knowledge of these other systems, or, more probably, had had a direct personal experience of the spiritual realities that these symbols represent.
6. A final point will be more easily recognised by all. The compilers of our system had an unparalleled knowledge of man's psychological and spiritual nature and needs, and they sought, both by explicit instruction and under a veil of symbolism, to show how these needs could be met.

It may be recognised that these qualities characterised those learned brethren who finally formulated the 1835 ritual from the accumulated mass of material they had at their disposal. But the question naturally arises – did they characterise them only, or also those brethren who selected and preserved, during the preceding 150 years, the various elements that were incorporated into the 1835 ritual? We have seen that B and J are found in masonry since at least the end of the seventeenth century; and also that of other details to be found at that time some (such as the FPOF) were retained but adapted to a different setting. We have seen, too, that the Noah legend appears to have been tried out, found to be inadequate, and rejected, while the Hiramic Legend was adopted some time prior to 1730 and has been retained ever since. It seems not unreasonable to assume that the selection was made deliberately and that the elements 'tried out' were retained or rejected according to whether or not they were adequate for an ultimate purpose that the selectors had in view. Can we form any reasonable conjecture as to who these selectors might have been and who preserved and transmitted the 'selected' elements?

There is a long-standing tradition that the Rosicrucians had a considerable if not a controlling influence in these matters, but this tradition has been consistently rejected by writers of the Authentic school on the grounds that there is no direct documentary evidence to support it. But it has to be borne in mind that members of the Rosicrucian Fraternity have never at any time publicly acknowledged such membership. This policy was at first adopted because it was a necessary precaution in view of the exigencies of the time; and in practice it has been perpetuated as an established tradition. There are, however, many historical facts which, in their cumulative effect, provide a considerable body of circumstantial evidence that suggests at least the possibility of such a Rosicrucian influence.

1. First there is their original manifesto, the *Fama Fraternitatis R∴C∴*, which was published in Cassel in 1614. This clearly shows that their aims and ideals were consonant with those of Freemasonry, that the Order was essentially Christian, and that the Kaballah had a basic place in their system of philosophy.
2. The *Fama* was widely studied in England and in Scotland during the seventeenth century. A manuscript transla-

tion, dated 1633, in the handwriting of Sir David Lindsay, who was created first Earl of Balcarres, is still in the library of the Earl of Crawford and Balcarres; and a small book by Archdeacon J. B. Craven, DD, on *The Esoteric Studies of Robert Leighton*, DD, who was Bishop of Dunblane from 1661 till 1672, states that the libraries of various noble Houses in Scotland also contain books of that period pertaining to such esoteric studies.

3. In 1652 there was published an English translation of the *Fama* by Thomas Vaughan who, though he 'denies' that he was a member of the Rosicrucian Brotherhood, was nevertheless steeped in their teachings, as is evidenced by his many other writings. There is, however, no evidence that he was a Freemason, but he is known at least to have met Elias Ashmole.

4. The Order is known to have been active in Europe during the eighteenth century, and there is very good reason to believe that it was then also active in England. Godfrey Higgins, in his *Anacalypsis*, says that a College of the Fraternity was still working in London in 1830. The continuity of the Rosicrucian Brotherhood during that period suggests a possible channel by which the results of successive generations of those concerned in the 'selection' of appropriate material could have been preserved and transmitted.

These facts and possible inferences therefrom do not prove any direct connection between Rosicrucianism and Freemasonry; but if they are taken all together, and if what is known of Rosicrucian teachings be correlated with what is stated in this paper about the development of our Ritual between 1696 and 1835, it must surely be agreed that such a connection was at least possible, and that brother R. F. Gould could have had quite adequate grounds for his statement, already quoted, that 'during the sixteenth and seventeenth centuries Kabalism and Rosicrucianism profoundly influenced many secret societies in Europe; and Freemasonry received no slight tinge from the Kaballistic pursuits of some of its adherents at that time'. In any case, one might ask those who refuse to accept, even as a working hypothesis, the possibility of such a connection, what alternative hypothesis they can offer that could more adequately and reasonably account for the wonderful perfection of our peculiar system – the completeness, the self-consistency, the symmetry, not only of the broad framework, but also of all the details that are so skilfully wrought into that framework. In any case, we are surely justified in exclaiming 'O, wonderful Masons! All Glory to the Most High!'

14
ON RITUAL

George Draffen

RITUAL HAS EXISTED in various forms for thousands of years, it is to be found all over the world wherever man has settled himself. Any doubt on this point can be at once eliminated by reading Sir James Fraser's *The Golden Bough*, a classic on the subject of early ritual and ceremonial.

When man ceased to be a wandering hunter and settled down to cultivate the ground he soon found that the vicissitudes of the weather seriously interfered with the growing of his crops and, therefore, with the supply of his food. Instead of attributing the vagaries of weather to natural phenomena he regarded them as an expression of naughty temper or serious displeasure by the various gods who made up his spiritual hierarchy. It was obviously necessary to propitiate the gods and consequently we find the rituals and ceremonials of Fertility Rites among the earliest recorded. Some were simple, others were complicated; some made use of human sacrifice, others were content with a symbolic object in place of the living victim; all were taken very seriously. As a variant of fertility rites in respect of the crops there were, of course, fertility rites in respect of flocks and herds of animals and, indeed, in respect of wives.

Among the early rituals and ceremonials we find the Initiation Rite. This was, and still is among the more primitive people of the world, one of the most important rites. When a young man reached puberty it was necessary to introduce him to his duties as a member of the tribe so that he could take a full part in its three principal activities – the obtaining of food, the defence of the tribe against its enemies, and the perpetuation of the tribe by the procreation of children. Many of these initiatory rites were both long and complicated, often lasting days and even weeks. They frequently involved trials of strength and stamina, long and dangerous journeys, the performance of some difficult task (such as bringing back the severed head of a member of an enemy tribe). Some of these tests have been carried forward in a symbolic form until one finds the severed head of an enemy becoming the rescuing of a damsel in distress by a postulant Knight.

As a general rule Initiation Rites were confined to the male members of the tribe, but there is evidence to show that there existed androgynous rites in which the females of the tribe were initiated into their duties, *ie*, the preparation of food, the making of clothing and domestic utensils and, possibly the most important, childbirth and the bringing up of children.

The numerous forms of early Initiation Rites are so varied that it is impossible to compare satisfactorily one ritual initiation with another.

As man developed a spiritual sense and created for himself a hierarchy of gods, before the rise of the three great monotheistic religions – Christianity, Judaism and Islam – he enveloped the worship of his gods with a variety of rituals and ceremonials. Some of these ceremonials have come down to us, but few in great detail. Some portions may have been carried over into the monotheistic religions when they began to arise.

It is interesting to observe that Christianity, Judaism and Islam all began as very simple creeds with few trappings in the services of worship. As time passed the services whether within a church, a synagogue or mosque began to grow more and more elaborate. In so far as Christianity is concerned the rise and development of the ritual ceremonial can most easily be comprehended in *The Shape of the Liturgy* by Dom Gregory Dix. Dix's book shows very clearly how the simple and primitive worship of the early Christian Church gradually developed into the highly complicated pattern of Pontifical

High Mass. I am not sufficiently acquainted with the ceremonials used in the synagogue or the mosque to be able to offer any similar development in Judaism and Islam, but it is possible that such exists.

With such a development as I have mentioned in the Roman Church, and considering how widely scattered were the little groups of early Christians, it is not surprising to learn that there were a wide number of variants on the central theme of the Christian worship. As the early Christian Church grew and coalesced into one or other of the two great branches (the Western Church and the Eastern Church) these variants became not only a stumbling block to intercommunication and intercommunion, but frequently a source of strife. In 1568 Pope Pius V (1504–1572) decreed that in the Western Church one standard form of Mass would be used by every church, cathedral and abbey unless it could be proved that another form of the Mass had been regularly celebrated for a period of one hundred years. The consequence of this decision is that only some three or four of the old forms of Mass still survive today, of which perhaps the best known is the Bessarabian Rite celebrated in Toledo in Spain. This idea of a standard ritual for church worship is, of course, also to be found in the *Book of Common Prayer* used by the Church of England. It is perhaps not commonly realised that the *Book of Common Prayer* is in fact part of an Act of Parliament and that it is technically quite illegal to use any other form of worship in any Parish Church in England. The English *Book of Common Prayer* has its variants which are to be found in the *Book of Common Prayer* used by the Episcopal Church in Scotland, the Episcopal Church in the United States of America and in the various Anglican Churches in the Commonwealth.

In so far as our masonic ritual is concerned it must be remembered that it is not a ritual for worship but a ritual for initiation into a brotherhood. The fact that there is within it a number of prayers does not of itself make it a ritual of worship. In the initiation rites of primitive tribes prayers to the local gods are frequently found and they have the same objective – to support the candidate spiritually through the trials required for his initiation and ultimate full membership of the tribe or the brotherhood.

An examination of all true rites shows that they have much in common though they may be expressed in different ways and sometimes apparently be absent. Among the common factors are Preparation, a Ritual Journey, a New Name, Refreshment, Symbolic Rebirth, a Reward and an Investiture with power or authority, coupled often with special clothing.

Preparation frequently takes the form of divesting the postulant of his normal clothing, either in part or in whole, and sometimes in clothing him with a special garment, usually white to symbolise purity. He is sometimes required to wash his hands; this again being a symbol of purity. His head may be covered and he may be blindfolded. It is interesting to note that as the postulant progresses toward the 'Higher Degrees' the hoodwink ceases to be used on the assumption that he is now, though not fully at least sufficiently, mentally advanced not to require this part of the preparation.

The Ritual Journey occurs in almost every degree and it is to be found in all the Mysteries going back through the centuries to those of which we have the earliest records. In the Mysteries of Egypt the ritual journey was long and distinctly perilous and many a postulant lost his life in attempting to accomplish it. Today there is, of course, no risk of this sort of thing, for the journey is purely symbolic. I might interpolate here that in the Scandinavian Rite the journey is certainly long, quite difficult and if not perilous at least more than a little disconcerting. The Ritual Journey may or may not involve symbolic dangers or sudden halts. It is sometimes not realised that the halts or stops made by the candidate during his circum-ambulation are intended to be danger points or testing points which he must overcome. It is important, too, to note the direction in which the ritual journey is taken. In most of our Masonic Degrees the journey is made clockwise round the lodge room, but there is at least one Degree in which the journey is made anti-clockwise or 'widdershins'. The expression 'widdershins' is an old term for death and witches and ghosts are, traditionally, supposed to travel from place to place in a widdershin or anti-clockwise direction. In the particular case which I have in mind the symbolism is not death directly, but rebirth following death.

The New Name does not occur in many of our Masonic Degrees. I am only familiar with two, but there may be others. In one of the two the new name is conveyed to the postulant in such a way that he, and he alone, is aware of what it is. This idea is very old and is still to be found in South Africa where many of the indigenous inhabitants still believe that for one person to know another person's *real* or true name is to have complete power and control over him. Thus while in common custom a man may refer to himself as Mr Odanga and be so called by his friends and relations that, in point of fact, is not his real name which he alone knows.

The factor of *Refreshment* occurs in at least two of our Masonic Degrees and in both cases the liquid part of the refreshment is wine. This refreshment is sometimes given in the middle of the ritual journey and sometimes at the end. There is also a possibility that it may be linked with the idea of Reward – being a reward of a minor nature for having got so far in the ceremony.

The factor of *Rebirth* is, of course, to be found in the Third Degree and it is also found in others. The symbolism can be as clear or as complicated as the postulant likes to make it, but basically, of course, it represents the New Man ready to undertake his full duties.

Reward and Investiture. I take these two together because they are generally so intermixed as to make it difficult to separate them accurately. In a sense any investiture with power and authority is in a way a reward for services rendered. The Investiture itself takes many forms; clothing with an apron, garbing with a robe, placing a crown or a special hat on the head, girding on a sword, putting a jewel on the breast and, perhaps the most ancient of all, placing a ring on the finger as a symbol of unity and binding the postulant to his brotherhood as it were in wedlock.

There is much about our rituals which I have left unsaid; there are common factors which I have not mentioned. This because I feel it undesirable to force my own views on the interpretation of any of these symbols which I have mentioned and because it is a good thing for each brother himself to search out and discover what the rituals of the various degrees of which he may be a member have to offer.

BOOKS FOR FREEMASONS

Books

We have been publishing masonic books for over 100 years including the well known EMULATION RITUAL. We always have a vast range of titles available and many are covered in our detailed book catalogue which is available upon request.

Write, telephone or call at our masonic showroom in Shepperton where you will be assured of a prompt and friendly service.

LEWIS MASONIC

Terminal House, Station Approach, Shepperton TW17 8AS. Walton-on-Thames 28950.